COG DAYS

Cog Days

*A Boy's Life and One Tragic
Summer on Mt. Washington*

Joseph W. McQuaid

PLAIDSWEDE PUBLISHING

Concord, New Hampshire

Designed and composed in Garamond Premier Pro with Gill Sans display at Hobblebush Books, Brookline, New Hampshire (www.hobblebush.com)

Printed in the United States of America

ISBN: 978-0-9962182-7-6
Library of Congress Control Number: 2017942659

Tim Lewis has the title of photo editor for this book, but he has been much more. Tim grew up at the Cog where his dad, Norman "Jitney" Lewis, was an engineer and confidante of Col. Arthur S. Teague. I am indebted to Tim for his help in discovering valuable pieces of Cog history, including some of Col. Teague's war records. I am indebted to Jitney for his humor and example. Thanks, too, to Bob and Shirley Kent for sharing photos.

Front cover Cog photo courtesy of the *Union Leader*
Back cover Cog photo courtesy of Lewis Family Collection

Published by:
PLAIDSWEDE PUBLISHING
P.O. Box 269 · Concord, New Hampshire 03302-0269
www.plaidswede.com

*Dedicated to Jitney and Tim Lewis
and Claire Dwyer, keepers of the flame.*

CONTENTS

FOREWORD

*Crawford Hassen at Cog Party stands in front of
his painting of a bear fleeing a forest fire.*

WHEN I THOUGHT OF WRITING THIS, years ago, it was to be a story of teenagers and young men and women who, over the course of a few post-World War II decades of the American Century, were lucky enough to spend their summers up in the White Mountains of New Hampshire, helping to run a century-old, steam-powered cog railway and related tourist attraction. It was an experience none of them would forget but one that time and circumstance have gradually erased, leaving just memories like my own.

Those who lived it are in a way like people lucky enough to have seen the Old Man of the Mountain before it toppled from its perch high above Franconia Notch in 2003.

Some are one in the same. One of my Mt. Washington Cog Railway colleagues, a southerner who remained in New Hampshire and became a successful banker, was so upset with the loss of the rock profile that he asked me to see that it was restored.

I had been named to a governor's commission to study what to do about the calamity. The Old Man was not only the state's symbol, it was in many ways its brand and its ethos.

My colleague's emotions couldn't let him see that having man try to restore the Old Man was like trying to bring back those Cog days of our youth.

The Old Man, seen by millions over two centuries, had fallen in the dead of night on a cold spring weekend. If anyone saw it happen, they never came forward. By contrast, many people have seen the cumulative changes that have erased the Cog of my youth. But there will come a day when no one who saw or experienced the old Cog is left to come forward.

Beyond recalling an exciting time for teenagers, this story is a remembrance and belated recognition for an extraordinary American whose own post-college summers were spent in those mountains and whose call to service in World War II changed his life, the lives of thousands under his command, and the Cog when he returned to it.

It is where he raised his family and provided for all those men, boys, and girls, and where he struggled and sweat to preserve an important working piece of history.

Arthur S. Teague's rise from the son of a southern widow to military prep school grad, Army Reserve officer and infantry battalion colonel who fought at Utah Beach and across Europe ought to be the stuff of legend. His commanding general called him "the bravest man in the United States Army."

It is not too much to say that Teague's actions in command under fire were instrumental in the swiftness of victory and in the saving of many lives.

But that "bravest man" phrase rattled around in my mind and puzzled me for a time in writing this story. It was not hyperbole. Teague was a brave man. But somewhere in my research, I had heard the line applied to Arthur Teague in a context other than war.

It took me awhile to recall its source. I had heard it from one of his longest-serving Coggers, in turn told to him by someone who had seen an example.

Art Teague, standing on the steeply pitched roof of a three-story building, calmly tacking down sections of the roof that were being ripped apart in one of the fierce winds that the mountains throw down upon mortals, just to remind them of who is boss.

And there had been another instance, too, where Teague's cool bravery came through on that mountain; when an employee at the summit hotel had armed himself with a knife and threatened others but who meekly came out of his room when Arthur Teague ordered him to do so.

Finally, this is a story of one terrible summer that took Teague's life and that of a daughter, saw the worst accident in the railway's history, and changed forever the Cog and those who loved it.

COG DAYS

Chapter 1

MOUNTAIN MEN

Four friends at ticket office. Left to right:
Joe McQuaid, Dave Koop, Gordon Champion, Norm Koop.

I WAS TOO YOUNG and too caught up in it at the time to understand that the Cog era I was entering in 1965 was already disappearing. I was vaguely familiar with Col. Teague's war experience. Many other Coggers my age knew none of it.

In my first summers, the Cog seemed a time and place of endless days of sharp blue skies that stretched in all directions from the summit of Mt. Washington (at 6,288 feet, it is the tallest peak in the northeastern United States). They soared across the Presidential Range and out over what seemed all of New Hampshire.

On the best days, from the summit, the outline of faraway cities (some said Montreal, others claimed Boston) and the Atlantic Ocean were said to be visible with the naked eye. Tourists were so numerous, and the ticket price so low, that double-headers (two trains making the trip at once) happened most days and triple headers several times a summer. When the nights did come, the stars were vast, and once or twice in the fall, the Northern Lights rolled across the sky like a multicolored sea.

We worked seven days a week all summer and could only have been happier if there were more. More days. More summers. It was a time and place where some very young men and even a few teenaged boys "qualified" to become train crewmen, even engineers, equal in status and responsibility to much older men, all of them operating the bone-crunching, deafening coal-fired steam engines that had been doing much the same thing in the same way for nearly 100 years.

It was a place where up to 56 passengers rode in a car that was slowly pushed rather than pulled up the steep slopes by the engine and then backed down behind it, entrusted to a brakeman who might be all of 16 or 17 and whose job it was to deftly and precisely wrestle and maneuver the car's chain-pulled brakes to keep its weight off the engine on the steep three-mile descent.

I often wondered if the typical Teddy Tourist and his family (all tourists were Teddys to us, or "goofers") had any clue as to the dangers involved in their ride and the trust they were placing in our young hands. For most, I think they did not. In fact, I think few among the Coggers had a true appreciation for the dangers inherent in their job.

The safety record was so spotless, or so we assumed, that not much thought was given to it. Only in doing reading for this memoir did I learn of a serious accident involving a runaway repair car that smashed into a passenger train, injuring 20 in 1946. In 1949, the year I was born, a locomotive snapped a cog gear and slid out of control for 1000 feet before the torn-up ties beneath it slowed and finally stopped it. There were no injuries.

As an engineer (a level of mechanical advancement to which my wife still marvels), I once lost a passenger car and its tourist load, if only temporarily. For safety reasons, the engine and car are not attached. I had let my fireman go back to braking for one trip. He had gotten nervous and brought the car to a stop while I was looking down the track as we went. When I looked back up, all I could see was fog. I had to bring the engine back up the mountain a few hundred feet before I could make out the car and my crewman, sitting on the outside platform, smoking a cigarette.

He waved and bid me hello, telling me of his confidence that I would "show up" eventually.

"What did you tell the passengers?" I asked.

"I told them it was standard procedure for you to go down first to check the track."

I found out much later that a similar thing had happened to a crew just a year or two before our mishap. I'm not sure if they had neglected to tie their bell cord, which ran from the car to a bell in the engine cab. It would ring the bell if the car and engine separated more than a few feet. Ours was not connected that day.

We were removed from a world before cell phones and Internet, and TV was miles away. Most news came to us from newspapers (including the one which I would later run) brought up to the Base Station each morning by Cliff Kenny, the ticket seller. We read it mostly for the Red Sox scores.

Kenny was one of the old-timers whom Art Teague faithfully looked after and to whom he was as loyal as he had been to his men under fire in Europe. Kenny had been an engineer but had been crippled by arthritis. He walked in pain and could barely open his fingers to tear off the tickets and reach into the wooden cash drawer worn smooth by years of service. But he had a job.

Other news came to us through the mail, in a Life or Time magazine, or in letters from home, bringing talk of the Beatles and Rolling Stones, of what the family was doing or of Vietnam casualties, and later of the Martin Luther King and Bobby Kennedy assassinations. Good and bad, and it was almost all good in my first years, the world was all "down below" us. We were up at the Base Station, with the tallest mountains in the northeastern United States looming over us, protecting us.

I see now how the Cog must have seemed like heaven on earth to Art Teague, especially coming back from the hell of combat. Did he dream of Jacob's Ladder or of the Lakes of the Clouds while he was fighting across France or holding on for dear life in the hell that was the Hürtgen Forest?

When the bad came to the Cog, it came in waves, particularly in that one horrible summer. It was not so much an intrusion from down below, although it started with one, but a series of interior blows that would crush the Teagues, taking two of their family and leaving a third mentally fragile; see the deadliest crash in the railway's history; and ultimately make some of us grow up much faster than we would have liked.

The Cog ownership has changed. The young crews that were so special to those of us who served on them have been replaced by retirees or seasonal workers who move to jobs at nearby ski areas or hotels in the winters.

Most jarring, the engines and fuel have been changed from the classic, canted steam boilers with their sooty coal fuel to quiet diesel engines running on recycled fats and looking like oversized, brightly-painted refrigerators tipped sideways.

The Mountain

God has apparently lived atop Mt. Washington since Indian times.

It was called Agiocochook, "at the mountains on the other side," as translated from the Algonquin. Abenakis, the local subset of that Indian group, thought it home of the Great Spirit. Few if any ventured to its summit until English (or Irish) settler Darby Field climbed it in June of 1642, with two Indians as guides.

More modern poets and politicians also referenced the Creator when speaking of New Hampshire's mountains.

Massachusetts' Ralph Waldo Emerson may have been tweaking New Hampshire native sons such as Daniel Webster when he wrote that, "The God who made New Hampshire taunted the lofty land with little men."

How ungracious.

Statesman Webster had lived before Emerson and is credited (the actual source and circumstance have never been found) with writing better of God and the men He made here.

"Men hang out their signs indicative of their respective trades; shoe makers hang out a gigantic shoe; jewelers a monster watch, and the dentist hangs out a gold tooth; but up in the Mountains of New Hampshire, God Almighty has hung out a sign to show that there He makes men."

Webster's reference was to the Old Man of the Mountain. Its foreboding profile jutted from the Cannon Cliffs in Franconia Notch for perhaps a thousand years. It was just a few miles below Mt. Washington.

It was still there when I worked at the Cog. It was on those Cannon Cliffs that one of those teen Cog crewmen, a son of U.S. Surgeon General Dr. C. Everett Koop, died in a climbing accident. The body of handsome young David Koop, a Dartmouth College student, dangled from a rope for hours before it could be retrieved. He was a brother of Cog engineer Norman Koop, who would marry Anne Teague of the owner's family and become a minister in part, some said, because of his brother's death.

Another brother, Alan Koop, became a college history professor and wrote a book about a German prisoner of war camp in Stark, N.H. Were those Germans captured as the result of Art Teague's army? The POWs were put to work as loggers helping to supply New Hampshire paper mills whose regular workers had, like Teague, gone off to fight in Europe. The Americans, of course, couldn't wait to return at the end of the war. Some of the POWs, however, didn't want to leave New Hampshire and became U.S. citizens.

The Rev. Norman Koop would find his home and life's work at a church in Woodstock, Vt., and minister to students at Dartmouth College, where his dad and brothers had studied. Norm would die of a heart attack doing something he loved, chopping firewood on a beautiful October day in 2015.

Some of the coal-fired steam engines that chugged and rattled up the Northeast's highest peak for more than a century were also given Indian names along with their official railroad numbers. The Number Two (or "the Deuce"), which I ran one summer, was the Ammonoosuc, which I knew as the name of the river that started at the grandly named but tiny Lakes of the Clouds on a saddle below Mt. Washington. Today, my Twitter handle is @deucecrew, which remains a puzzle to politicians and pundits.

The Ammonoosuc's meaning, in Abenaki, is a small, narrow fishing place. Whether those who named the engine knew it or not, it fit nicely with where it and several of the Cog's engines were made. The Amoskeag Manufacturing Company, just below the Amoskeag Falls in my home city of Manchester, was world famous for its textiles and machinery. Amoskeag means place of many fish.

The 9 engine was the Waumbek. "Waumbekketmethna" translates to white (Waumbekkett) mountains (methna). The Abenaki word waube-ghiket-amadinar means "white greatest mountain."

But take some of these names and meanings with a dose of skepticism as different sources have different interpretations. A 1916 book, "Chronicles of the White Mountains," questions early poets and settlers who insisted that Agiocochook translated to "The Place of the Great Storm Spirit of the Forest."

"Chronicles" quotes an earlier scholar of the Algonquin language as concluding that no element of any Algonquin word meant "great" or "spirit" or "forest." "Chronicles" author Frederick W. Kilbourne notes that the

Indians may have been trying to translate English words, such as "White Mountains," into something approximating their language.

Even the reason for calling them "white" is open to debate. Some thought that the snow that blankets some peaks for up to eight months of the year provided the name. But Kilbourne wrote that "Christall hill" was referenced in a 1628 "A Voyage into New-England." Seen far off, the high peaks with no moss to cover their rocks appear white.

Whatever their names, those great white mountains began attracting tourists as far back as the days of pioneer Abel Crawford and his son and daughter-in-law, Ethan Allen Crawford and Lucy Crawford.

Their rustic lodgings near the Crawford Notch sheltered poets, hunters and other travelers eager to see the mountains' beauty. And the father and son would blaze the first tourist trails to the top of Agiocochook. One trail would become known as Crawford's bridle path, though "path" hardly defines the steep slopes over which it traveled.

In a book written in his name by his wife, Lucy, Ethan Allen Crawford tells of taking to the Mt. Washington summit two men who gave the surrounding peaks the names that became known collectively as the Presidential Range.

Ethan Allen Crawford often had to dissuade eager visitors from making the climb or, in some cases, bodily carry them down thereafter. An illustration in Lucy Crawford's book shows her husband carrying a woman, seemingly comfortably seated on his right shoulder, as he descends the steep slope known as Jacob's Ladder. It was on this route, from his hotel at Fabyans, that Ethan Allen Crawford blazed a second tourist trail, which would later be followed as the route for the Cog.

In 1852, a few years after Crawford's death, Sylvester Marsh and a friend took that path up Mt. Washington and nearly died in the attempt. But unlike others, who merely thanked God (or Crawford, or both) for surviving, Marsh decided there must be a better, safer way to the summit than by hiking or riding a horse up the dizzying and rocky trail.

Marsh was from Campton, New Hampshire, and was a nationally known businessman and innovator. He had made his fortune as a meat-packer, including helping turn a 300-person village into the boomtown of Chicago. After his near-death experience on the trail, he went to work on his mountain-climbing idea. He also became acquainted with Herrick Aiken.

Aiken, an inventor and mechanical engineer from Franklin, had patented a process for a mountain-climbing cog railway, although even he wasn't the first to do so. Aiken envisioned a cog railway going up Mt. Washington; he even built a model but was dissuaded from building the real thing himself by railroad men who were said to think it impractical and expensive.

How much of Aiken's acumen went into Marsh's plan is unclear, but it is known that the two visited several times. Marsh would then unveil his own cog model and begin selling stock to raise money for his plan.

In 1858, Marsh asked the state legislature for a right of way up the mountain for a railway. They might have been impressed with his business skills, but some doubting legislators laughingly approved Marsh's charter, adding that he could have that right of way all the way to the moon.

It would take Marsh several years to perfect his version of the toothed cog wheel that pulls the engine up the steep inclines. And it took much of that time, too, to build the railroad bed and lay the track up the mountain. They first had to carve a trail from Fabyans that was wide enough for yokes of oxen to haul in equipment, supplies and rails.

The line was begun in 1865 but not finished to the summit until July 3, 1869. The farther right of way to the moon has yet to be exercised.

Two Teagues

Henry Teague didn't shoot for the moon when he acquired the Cog. But he was a showman and a risk-taker. He was born on Mt. Desert Island, Maine, and had made a fortune in Florida land deals during the Roaring Twenties. When the Wall Street crash came in 1929, Henry told a newspaper reporter that he had lost a million dollars. Better luck was with him back in New Hampshire.

The Boston and Maine Railroad had owned the Mt. Washington Cog Railway since the 1880s. In the early days of the Depression, it was eager to dump non-performing assets. The Cog was one of them. The B&M spur line that had shuttled wealthy passengers right up to the Base Station was rusting. The Depression was clobbering tourism.

Henry Teague had never owned a railroad, but he was friends with B&M president Edward French and French's assistant, Lawrence F. Whitmore. They made Henry an offer hard to refuse.

They would sell him the Cog and its base station and summit property for $100,000. Henry said he didn't have it. They said the B&M would loan him the money. Henry said he needed working capital. They put $10,000 in the bank for him. The B&M went even further, allowing train crewmen who wanted to take a break from their regular jobs to work summers at the Cog.

"The Colonel," a title Henry Teague he had been given years earlier as an honorific by New Hampshire Gov. John Winant, bought the Cog. He added more trips, reduced fares, and tirelessly promoted the railway throughout New Hampshire, which already relied heavily on tourism.

He also introduced an end-of-the-season profit-sharing plan that helped return loyal and competent workers to the Cog each summer and helped pay their tuitions in the fall and winter. (When I was there in the mid-60s, a season-ending bonus still existed.)

The future Col. Art Teague met the Hon. Col. Henry Teague in the fall of 1931. Family lore has Art hitchhiking and being picked up by the older colonel on a road in South Carolina. More likely, Art, then in his senior year at Clemson University studying engineering, was there when the older colonel was making one of his periodic recruiting trips through southern colleges.

The two were unrelated or perhaps distantly related by blood but would be bound together by love for a mountain, a steam railway and a way of life.

The Boston and Maine had used its regular employees to staff the Cog. That was one of the reasons why it wanted to unload the line during the Depression. Henry Teague needed to recruit students to take the places of these men. Some he found close by in Hanover, N.H., at his alma mater, Dartmouth College. For others, he would stop at colleges as he made his way to Florida each winter.

Henry's running into Art Teague was one of those chance things that change history. Henry's running into a young Philadelphia nurse a few years later was also by chance. But when he introduced Ellen Crawford to his protégé, Art, he knew what he was doing.

Arthur Simpson Teague was born May 25, 1910, in Graniteville, South Carolina. (Those familiar with New Hampshire know its nickname as the Granite State.) The only son of a South Carolina country doctor, Art grew up in a tiny town tucked up against South Carolina's border with Georgia. It is now part of the Augusta, Georgia, metropolitan area. It is known as home to the first large-scale cotton mill in the American South, and it sits just 227 feet above sea level.

Art Teague must have sometimes marveled at the distance he would travel from there to northern New England's peaks, and then to the battle-fields of Europe and back.

Dr. Teague died when Art was six years old. When Art was 13, his mother relocated herself, Art, and his sister to nearby Augusta. The city was home to what was then known as the Richmond County Military Academy, a military prep school. It was all-male and had been training young cadets since just after the Civil War, or about the time the Cog was under construction.

Whether young Arthur was drawn to the military or it was his family's choice isn't known. Soldiering was certainly an esteemed profession in the antebellum South. Arthur clearly took to it, spending four years at the academy. Perhaps its structure appealed to a fatherless boy. It was the beginning of his learning the skills and discipline that he would put to good use 20 years on in Europe.

The military theme continued after prep school. Art returned to his native South Carolina, entering Clemson University in 1928. Then as now, it was famed for its engineering curriculum, and Art would be graduated four years later with a Bachelor of Science in engineering. Like his military training, the engineering curriculum would also serve him and those he would command in the coming war.

Art entered the ROTC (Reserve Officers Training Corps) program and stayed with it all four years at Clemson, ending as cadet captain his senior year. He was commissioned a second lieutenant in the Army

Reserves and would spend the 1932 summer after his graduation at Fort Moultrie in Charleston, S.C. The next year, 1933, he came north to work for Henry Teague.

Henry had never married. His Cog employees became his family. He was impressed with Art's work ethic and mechanical skills. Art returned south after his first Cog summer to study for his master's degree in engineering at the University of South Carolina, and then headed back to Mt. Washington the next year. He was following a pattern Henry had ingrained in many southern college students.

But unlike others content to shovel coal and run the engines for their pay, Art applied his engineering skills to different facets of the Cog. He installed a Pelton water wheel driven by water piped from Franklin Brook, which roared down the mountain to the base.

The power ran a water pump delivering eight gallons a minute to the summit house tank. It also provided lights for the Base Station and power for its machine shops, where parts were made, repaired and maintained. Art then turned his attention to what had been the intractable problem of switching trains on the complicated cog rack system.

"The most revolutionary improvements (sic) on the cog railway was the installing of turnouts at the Base Station and the Waumbek Tank in 1941 and at the Gulf Tank the following year," read a Cog booklet published during Art Teague's years.

Up to that time, like all other cog railways, this road had been one-track. Some trains would run to Halfway platform, where passengers would be transferred to another train that would be housed at the summit.

Finding a way for trains to pass each other, thus greatly expanding trip capacity, was a tough issue. Working with Lawrence Richardson, who had been chief mechanical engineer for the previous owner, the Boston and Maine Railroad, Arthur Teague devised a turn-out mechanism that permitted the cog apparatus to cross over and to turn out and level off safely and satisfactorily on the mountainside.

"Although the device looks complicated, it can be worked easily by one man. It requires about 18 moves to operate the design, but it takes less than five minutes for the shift over and the passing of the trains."

According to the booklet, an engineer from the Panama Canal was sent up to secure blueprints. Similar turnouts were later used at the canal, permitting engine "mules" to pass one another along the canal's banks.

Art had been working for Henry Teague for a few years when the two found themselves in Florida in the winter of 1940-41. Also in Miami Beach was Ellen Crawford, a young and outgoing nurse from Philadelphia. Ellen had been in the White Mountains herself. She and a friend were private nurses to a well-to-do elderly woman who summered at the Mountain View House (now the Mountain View Grand Resort and Spa) in Whitefield and spent winter in Miami Beach.

Ellen, off duty and having a drink by herself at a hotel bar, caught the eye of Henry Teague. He came to her table, bought her a drink and, according to her memoir, the two talked about beautiful Key Biscayne sunsets.

Henry said she would have to come to the summit of Mt. Washington to see the best sunsets. He also told her he would like to bring young Art Teague around the next day to meet her.

She wrote that she was initially put off by the striking birthmark (a large port wine stain) that crossed the bridge of his nose. Today a simple laser treatment would eliminate it. But in Art Teague's time, such a mark could forever define a person. For Art Teague, the birthmark defined him as someone whose beauty and mettle were much deeper than his skin.

As for Ellen Crawford, she was captivated by Arthur Teague's hazel eyes, firm handshake, and courtly manner. The two began a courtship.

In March of 1941, with war raging in Europe and now on the near-horizon for America, President Franklin D. Roosevelt was pressing to build our military and reinstate a military draft against considerable opposition by Americans who didn't want us in another world war.

The previous summer, FDR had named stalwart Republicans Henry Stimson and Frank Knox as his Secretary of War and Secretary of the Navy, respectively. FDR knew what he was doing. If he were to rally the country, he was going to need a bipartisan cabinet.

For their perceived political apostasy, however, Stimson and Knox were nearly drummed out of the GOP at its 1940 presidential convention in Philadelphia. Knox, incidentally, was the owner and publisher of the Manchester Union Leader and had been the GOP's vice presidential nominee in 1936. Before that, he had fought up Kettle Hill, Cuba, as one of Teddy Roosevelt's Rough Riders and would be instrumental in TR's ill-fated 1912 try to regain the White House. He became an Army major in the First World War, overseeing an artillery detachment. Knox was also my father's boss as owner of the Chicago Daily News foreign news service.

Lt. Art Teague was called to active duty in 1940. He would spend his entire active military career with the 22nd Infantry Regiment, 4th Infantry Division, mustering out as regimental commander in 1946. (He would stay with the U.S. Army Reserve into the 1960s.)

Art by this time was going steady with Ellen, on his infrequent leaves. With Pearl Harbor having brought America into the war, they decided to marry in early 1942, knowing that he would be shipping out at some point soon. Henry Teague served as best man for the man to whom he had introduced his bride and who had become a son to him.

Art and Ellen's first child, Jane, was born in 1943. That winter, the regiment shipped out to England. D-Day on the beaches of Normandy and the war to free Europe lay dead ahead.

Chapter 2

THE BRAVEST MAN

Col. Arthur S. Teague led fighting men across Europe and returned to run and then own the Mt. Washington Cog Railway. (Courtesy of Dartmouth College Library)

IT IS DIFFICULT TO FATHOM, especially at a time now so far removed, the depths of individual skill, bravery and daring that so many Americans demonstrated during the war. But what others in the fight had to say about an individual while the war was all around them is a good measure. What they said about Arthur Teague was extraordinary.

One of them was U.S. Army Captain Walter E. Marchand, who wrote of Teague in a "D-Day Doctor's Diary" published after the war.

Capt. Marchand would cross the English Channel with Teague on the HMS Gauntlet, a transport ship, hit the Utah Beach landing with him, and spend much of the next two months observing Teague while tending to the wounded and dying.

A "Diary" entry from July 2: "Col. Teague and all the Battalion staff officers talk to the enlisted men—a pep talk—sensible and clear. Col. Teague is a great leader and we all look up to him—clear head and not foolhardy—brave and never demanding the impossible."

Other officers didn't rate such praise from Marchand. In another entry, he recalls with disdain an unnamed officer threatening his command should an objective not be met.

But in his praise for Art Teague, the doctor was not alone. The regimental history, written at the war's end, said of him: "A great soldier, excellent technician, leader of men and loyal friend of both his officers and men, Art Teague was loved and respected by the Twenty-Second Infantry Regiment as were few men."

Major General Raymond O. Barton, commander of 4th Infantry Division, would say of Teague, "in my estimation, the bravest man in the United States Army."

And Col. C.T. Lanham, the regimental commander, wrote: "He could command a division with distinction. He has a miraculous eye and feel for terrain, and is the most competent leader in battle I have ever known."

Teague's rise in rank and responsibility was itself remarkable. Within 22 months, he had been promoted from lieutenant to lieutenant colonel and given command of the 3rd battalion. He would lead them ashore on June 6, 1944, as part of the Allies' massive land assault on Hitler's Fortress Europe.

Landing at Utah Beach that morning, Teague was immediately summoned by Gen. Theodore Roosevelt, Jr. President Teddy Roosevelt's namesake and eldest son should not have been on the beach at all. In his mid-50s, he had a bad heart, unknown at the time. A wound received in World War I required him to use a cane to walk.

But he had cajoled 4th Division Commander "Tubby" Barton into letting him lead the Utah landings for the Americans.

Ironically, this Roosevelt had strongly opposed the pro-interventionist policies of his distant cousin, President Franklin Delano Roosevelt. But he did not resist or resign his commission when FDR had him called to active duty in 1941.

Roosevelt would die from a heart attack within a few weeks of the Normandy landing. (His grave at the American cemetery in Normandy is shared with his younger brother, Quentin, whose plane had been shot down in France in World War I. Authorities located his grave and now the two brothers rest together.)

In Otto Preminger's movie "The Longest Day," Gen. Roosevelt is portrayed by Henry Fonda, who memorably discovers that his troops have been put ashore miles from their designated zone. With his walking stick, he points up the beach and says that's where they should be. In the actual incident, one of those to whom he was speaking was Arthur Teague.

Attorney Jack Middleton, who would represent the Cog and serve on Teague's board of directors, said Teague spoke little of the war. He did say Teague told him of his interaction with Gen. Roosevelt.

Teague, Middleton recalled, said, "Roosevelt almost appeared to have a death wish the way he stood up with bullets whizzing all around."

Col. Teague, in a remarkable after-action report, told of his encounter with Roosevelt and of his subsequent actions that day and the next. They would earn him the Silver Star.

In his matter-of-fact way, Teague's map-reading ability is illustrated, as is his coolness under fire.

"We started up the beach and I hollered back to everybody and got them dissembled because I saw two men who were lost on mines. I stayed on the sand dunes to see if I could identify my location on the map. Standing with my back to the water, looking inland, a little bit to my right front was the little round windmill or silo standing up which I had observed on aerial photographs and panoramic views of the beach before, which gave me the immediate location of where we were."

He was so concentrated on his observations that he seemed oblivious to the firing around him.

"I tried to get higher on the sand dunes, but someone yelled at me that snipers were firing and for me to come down."

Teague led his men for more than 48 hours straight, advancing up from the beachhead as far as possible and continuing to witness death all around him.

"I went with a battalion staff behind K Company. I started wading in water up to my waist, and in some places, up to my armpits. A long column of men was wading through the water. A sniper got a man just ahead of me. He lay for most of the whole night because he couldn't be evacuated."

It was only the beginning of what Teague and his men would face and how the quiet young southerner would inspire and lead them during that summer.

In the space of several weeks, Teague's actions would lead to him winning the Distinguished Service Cross (considered second only to the Medal of Honor), the United Kingdom's Distinguished Service Order (presented to him by Field Marshall Bernard Law Montgomery), France's Croix de Guerre, and the Silver Star.

Teague's battalion also received a Presidential Unit Citation for extraordinary heroism and outstanding performance.

On June 17, Dr. Marchand's "Diary" notes that the force was advancing on Montebourg.

"As we get close meet up with a lot of artillery—it is raining hard all day.

Col. Teague is told to take the town in A.M.—but sees no need to since he feels Jerries will 'beat it' when 8th and 12th reach objectives—and so it proves to be. We sit outside of Montebourg all day—getting a lot of artillery, and as darkness falls we get the word to move—we surge thru blazing Montebourg—and make for the outskirts—we are to bivouac in a field with mines in it—have to test the ground myself before letting the boys come in—(the lot of an officer is tough—he has to lead the way). Start digging in—almost finish my slit trench when we get orders to move. Many mines encountered—several Jeeps blown."

This was all part of the Allies' fight to secure the Cotentin Peninsula from the Germans.

At one point, Teague and his battalion were cut off from their division overnight, with only spotty radio contact with their main force. Dr. Marchand, showing his own bravery under fire, managed with one aide to hitch rides on two tanks, which broke through the enemy lines.

Marchand found Col. Teague directing the fight. He also counted 67 wounded GIs spread over three fields.

He calmly went to work and "amputated a hand and plugged a few bleeding chest cases."

On June 25, Dr. Marchand watched Teague and Gen. Roosevelt observe American dive-bombers hitting Cherbourg, which would soon fall to the 4th Infantry.

The Clemson engineer may have also had a hand in how the Americans solved the problem of the boucage or hedgerow country whose thick earthen walls were stopping tanks from advancing. Teague would tell friend and Cogger Norm "Jitney" Lewis that it was one of Teague's men who came up with the idea to weld steel prongs onto the front of tanks to slice through the hedgerows.

From June to November, Teague miraculously remained the only American brigade commander in the entire theatre of war who had not been killed or wounded in action. His luck would not hold.

His division was assigned to the Hurtgen Forest campaign. It has been called the U.S. military's bloodiest battle since the Wilderness campaign of the Civil War. The comparison is appropriate. In both battles, incessant shelling caused the bulk of casualties. Author Robert Sterling Rush notes that the 22nd Infantry attacked on Nov. 16 and left the forest on Dec. 3. "During these eighteen days, the regiment lost 2,805 soldiers or 86 percent of its assigned strength." He goes on to explain, "Casualties were heavier than usual for the leaders and veterans, partly because experience counted little against artillery fire. Heavy shelling killed the wounded veteran and rookie indiscriminately."

Teague was wounded by artillery fire on the second day. (His counterpart in the 1st Battalion, Major Hubert Drake, was killed the same day.) His widow wrote later that Teague was too modest to disclose the nature of his wounds, but other family members believe he was hit in the leg and shoulder. He was transferred to England but would return to active duty as executive officer of the 22nd Regiment.

Teague's fortune may have been better than he might have thought at the time. The 4th Division was so chewed up in the Hurtgen campaign that it was reassigned thereafter to what was thought to be a quiet area in the Ardennnes. It became better known as the Battle of the Bulge.

In "Hell in Hurtgen Forest," Rush notes of Teague:

"He had joined the 3d Battalion in 1940 as a 2d Lieutenant and had never left, rising in rank from platoon leader to battalion commander. Teague had landed with his battalion in the first wave on Utah Beach and was one of the few officers who had never been wounded. A topographical engineer by profession, Teague would look at the map from every angle for about fifteen minutes and then issue very precise orders. Both his executive officer, Major James Kemp, also a native of South Carolina, and Captain Oscar Willingham, the battalion operations officer, were products of the pre D-Day regiment and ROTC graduates."

My fellow Cogger Steve Christy said he once heard Arthur Teague speak, not of the war, but of knowing the writer Ernest Hemingway during the war, possibly in Paris. That makes sense, as Hemingway had hooked up in Paris with Teague's 22nd Infantry commanding officer Col. C.T. "Buck" Lanham, who had called Teague the "most competent leader in battle I have ever known."

Teague may have also connected briefly with Hemingway in the Hurtgen Forest battle, which Hemingway would later use for his novel, "Across the River and into the Trees."

Hurtgen would devastate not just Teague's regiment but the entire 4th Division, inflicting more than 5,000 battle casualties. The 22nd had 391 casualties, including Teague and 27 other officers, during the battle's first three days.

Hemingway, in "Across the River," writes:

"Well anyway this regiment was rebuilt as American regiments always are by the replacement system...It boils down, or distills, to the fact you stay in until you are hit badly or killed or go crazy and get section eighted... We got a certain amount of replacements but I can remember thinking that it would be simpler, and more effective, to shoot them in the area where they de-trucked, than to have to try to bring them back from where they would be killed and bury them."

(Hemingway, considered by many war correspondents as more braggart than brave reporter, may have stolen that description from one of his wives, Martha Gelhorn, who had used it in her own war novel, "Point of No Return.")

Coincidentally, another writer was in the 4th Army in the Hurtgen front, although not in Teague's regiment. J.D. Salinger, who would find his own post-war peace in the New Hampshire countryside, worked on short stories during lulls in the fighting with his 12th Regiment.

Home

Mustered out as commander of the regiment in 1946, Art was ready for new challenges but also longing, I imagine, for the peace and familiar surroundings at Mt. Washington. Reuniting with Ellen and their toddler, and with a second baby as well, he enrolled in the University of South Carolina Law School. He had completed less than a semester when Henry Teague wrote, asking him to return to the Cog.

In her book, Ellen Teague writes that she told Art she would be happy with whatever decision he made. It was clear that the mountain and the Cog and Henry were all calling him. Ellen said that was fine with her. Years later, a daughter would remember her mother confiding that she had not been all that enthusiastic. But, after the hell of war, it is easy to see why the mountains of New Hampshire must have appealed so to Art Teague.

As Art went north, Ellen, pregnant with a third child, went home to Philadelphia. Art's letters to Ellen explained his efforts at trying to rebuild the Cog and its seasonal staff. The operation had been closed during the war years (it had done the same for one year during World War I) and was just now reopening.

Art spent weeks driving through New Hampshire and Vermont, looking up veteran engineers and recruiting new hires. He was able to pay just 80 cents an hour but, as he wrote to Ellen, he did better for Mike Boyce. The legendary engineer, who had worked at the Cog since at least 1909, came back for the princely wage of $1.20 an hour. (That was more, in 1946, than I received in 1965.)

Art Teague, followed soon by his growing family, settled into familiar surroundings, residing with Henry in "the Hut," a large and comfortable two-story log house whose upper porches faced Mt. Washington. Life was good.

George Trask knew both Teagues. He had been hired by the old colonel and served not only as a railway hand but as Henry's chauffeur and help-mate. Henry's "colonelcy" was honorary, but the old man had been in the military. He was a private in the Army National Guard and was ordered up for service in the Spanish-American war.

George Trask's most memorable trip driving the old colonel was to a 50th year reunion of Spanish-American veterans at the state capital of Concord. George says Henry was among the most plastered at the event.

Henry Teague died in 1951. Some thought he would leave the railway to his general manager and namesake. Some among Art Teague's family and friends thought it was a sure thing. But he had willed the property to his alma mater, Dartmouth College. The college had loaned Henry the money needed to repair the Cog after the 1938 New England hurricane that had ripped up Jacob's Ladder and other trestles. The storm had been so strong that sea brine scooped up by the wind off the Connecticut coast was found caking windows in Vermont.

Henry Teague had graduated from Dartmouth in 1900 and was its first graduate from the new Amos Tuck Business School the next year. The loan was still outstanding, and Henry's will also bequeathed sums of money to Dartmouth. The Cog had to pay those as well.

Ken Randall, longtime Cog bookkeeper, would work for both Henry and Art. He said it was assumed that Henry had been steadily paying the principal debt he owed Dartmouth. But it had only been interest on the loan.

Dartmouth College was happy to have Art Teague continue to run the Cog. It didn't really want to be in the railway business and, in 1962, Art was able to buy the railway. The college also leased him the Summit House hotel, which in 1964 would become the property of the State of New Hampshire, also sold by Dartmouth.

Randall says he doesn't know where Art found the money to pay the college. But the terms may have been generous. As with the Boston and Maine Railroad unloading the Cog to Henry Teague, Dartmouth seemed eager to do likewise with Art. The Cog Railway, where Art Teague had worked since his college days and for which, one could say, he had fought a war, was finally his. The joy of ownership was tempered by the continuing challenges of tough work, the constant fight against Mother Nature, and low profit margins in a seasonal business in a sometimes hostile climate.

Art and Ellen were also having more children. After Jane and Margie came Frances (Fanny) and Anne, and then Lucy and Charlie.

A Cogger who worked some of those years (1958-1962) remembers the Teagues as a "fine and energetic family...ambitious for themselves and their children—each in their own way."

Kevin McKinney had grown up in the same Philly neighborhood where the Teagues lived and was friends with Jane. He recalled it as a pleasure and privilege to work and learn at the Cog. It was only later in life, "when I began to have management responsibilities of my own that I realized how much they were able to accomplish amid the many variables at play—HR, finance, government relations, politics, weather, marketing, tourism promotion, scheduling maintenance, innovation—it just goes on."

That was the thing about Art and Ellen Teague. To outsiders, and even to the youngsters whom they hired, fed and watched out for each summer, they made their business seem fun. Looking back 50 years, McKinney said, "it's hard to fathom how they did it all—moving back and forth from PA to NH, raising a family, dealing with issue after challenging issue."

Jitney Lewis remembers times when there were still more tourists wanting to ride the Cog than there were crew members to assist. More than once, he said, a brakeman who thought he was on his last trip down for the day would find Art Teague serving as brakeman on an upcoming train at the Waumbek switch. Teague would then trade places and brake the descending train.

Like many Coggers, McKinney heard nothing of the war from Col. Teague, but he was well aware of Arthur's reputation as a soldier. "His leadership skills, focus and drive were apparent though. Now these many years later, I wish I had asked him about his service and his experiences but my hunch is that I would not have learned much since humility was also one of Arthur's admirable traits."

"One amazing aspect of Art," McKinney noted, "was that he always seemed to be energetic, positive, oriented to solving problems, and taking the time to 'guide and lead' so many young pups who often needed the guiding and the leading, and sometimes a swift kick too—but he never stooped to that nor did he seem upset."

Chapter 3

FIRST SUMMER

Richard "Tricky" Tirrell fired the No. 1 engine for Joe Long.

I WAS 16 AND HAD NEVER BEEN AWAY FROM HOME without family for more than a night's sleepover at a cousin's. I had never gone to summer camp. I had known few boys outside of my small town of Candia until attending high school in Manchester, the biggest city in our small state of New Hampshire.

I was ambivalent about going away. A new golf course had opened at what had been a dairy farm down the road from my parents' home. I had worked a few weeks the previous summer helping to build it, and I thought there might be caddying or other opportunities now.

My father ran our Sunday newspaper at the time and had published some stories about Col. Arthur Teague and the Cog Railway. And dad knew of Teague's wartime exploits.

My father decided I should go to work there. Years before, he had decided my older brother would work a summer job away from home as a busboy at a resort hotel. Years before that, he had himself worked summer jobs away from home, at Massachusetts beach hotels and as an office boy for the Boston newspaper for which his own father had been an editor.

As for the Cog, my father, B.J., told me it was a place with trains. He told me I liked trains, which was true, but the model trains that I liked ran on a tabletop in our house and had been used much more often by my father than by me. But when an older boy on our road heard of my good fortune, he was envious, so I was intrigued. He knew of the Cog, he said, and had always wanted to run the trains there and, boy, was I lucky. Turns out, he was right.

My parents drove me up at the start of that first summer, 1965. It was a three-hour-plus trip in the days before Interstate 93 made it through the mountains, cutting considerable travel time and also damaging many smaller tourist attractions along the old Route 3. What would be good for destination resorts and major attractions like the Cog would end up killing many small businesses.

As we pulled into the Cog's Base Station, with its smell of sulfurous coal smoke, a bell ringing, a shrill steam whistle bouncing back from the surrounding slopes, and a train ascending, my mother suddenly remembered that her parents had been here once.

Vague on details, she recalled only that there had been some sort of accident and her parents and others had been forced to leave their train and walk down the track.

I would find out later that this had been a famous and deadly incident, the only one to involve a non-Cogger before I worked there. In this case, it was a Boston photographer who was killed while another photographer was injured. The engineer, with the perfect New England name of Jack Frost, had to jump for his life, along with his son, and the fireman.

It had begun as a publicity stunt.

"Old Peppersass" originally had the much more poetic name of "Hero." It was the Cog's first engine and had been used in the railway's construction. It had gained its nickname from its long smoke stack's resemblance to the shape of a condiment bottle in use at the time.

Peppersass had been on loan to various expeditions and then had been lost track of before a Lancaster, N.H., minister, Guy Roberts (the same man who would help prolong the life of the Old Man of the Mountain profile), helped bring it back to New Hampshire. It was restored at the Boston and Maine repair yard in Concord and then sent back to the mountain.

It was to be used in a 1929 publicity climb recognizing the Cog's 60th anniversary. It would then be formally retired and placed on permanent display at the base of the mountain. On the big day, July 20, 1929, six trainloads of VIPS, including Gov. Charles Tobey, went chugging up the mountain in advance of Old Peppersass. It was a big day for New Hampshire. A national governors' conference had just concluded in Rhode Island, and a half dozen chief executives had come north to take the Cog trip and then dine with Tobey at the Crawford House.

My mother's father was head of the state Department of Motor Vehicles at the time. The DMV didn't oversee railroads, but it ran what became the state police, so he was sort of a big deal. Thus he and my grandmother being included among the guests.

The engine, by prearrangement, stopped its climb about two-thirds of the way up. It then began its slow descent. But on Jacob's Ladder, the line's steepest trestle, a cogwheel tooth snapped, jolting Peppersass violently. Engineer Frost tried the handbrake, to no avail. The engine picked up speed as it came crashing back down, ripping up ties as it did so. Luck or perhaps foresight had the trains full of VIP passengers ascending before Peppersass.

As my mother recalled it, her parents and others had to climb back down the track. Newspaper accounts of the day report that initially the VIP trains didn't know of the accident, which was below their sight line. As the trains proceeded back down, however, they noticed the torn up track. On Jacob's Ladder, they stopped. Below lay the dead man and the injured.

Somehow, passengers in the car closest to the scene were able to climb down to the rocks below, where they waited until the engines got up enough steam to bring them to the summit. Whether my grandparents were among the ones fit enough to have climbed down, or were with the others who waited for bus transport at the top, I do not know. I do know that it was nice of my mother to share that little memory with me just as I was about to start work at this strange and somewhat scary new place.

With the unsettling Peppersass memory imparted to me, my parents had lunch with Art and Ellen Teague in the Marshfield dining room. I am guessing my dad and Col. Teague talked World War II memories and battles, probably more from my father's side of the table than Art's. For decades after the war, B.J. enjoyed hearing from the men he had covered and reconnecting with the battles fought.

I don't recall exactly what I was doing while they dined, but I guess I was being shown around the premises, wondering what train would be mine to drive. Then, with a wave and a handshake, my parents were off. There would be no calls home, to say hi or yell for help. The nearest phone was a pay booth miles away at Fabyans, or miles up at the summit house.

My first week wasn't fun. In fact, it was miserable. Like others before and after me, I was quickly informed that I would be working at the Marshfield snack bar. Trains? That might come in later summers, if I made the grade.

The isolation made those first weeks even worse. I was shown my living quarters, the top bunk of a small bedroom in what was called the Boys' Dorm. This made it clear it wasn't the Girls' Dorm, where resided the small group of teenaged girls who served as waitresses at the restaurant and lunch counter or in the adjoining gift shop.

Boys in the dorm were generally younger, and newer to the Cog, than the residents of the imposing Men's Boarding House, a three-story affair for which the term ramshackle may have been created. Presumably, things were less rowdy in the boys' dorm, but certainly no quieter. It sat at the lower end of the base camp, which put it below the mechanical shops and the dump but right next to the pumping station that supplied water to the summit when the Franklin Brook was too low to power the Pelton waterwheel. The thing shut down in the evening but otherwise its loud, monotonous cranking was a daily affair.

It was at the pumping station that I first spied Crawford Hassen, a descendant, he claimed, of the mountain men who had settled the area and for whom Crawford Notch was named. This would also have made him a distant relation to Ellen Crawford Teague, something he liked to tweak her kin about.

I would come to know and like Crawford, but at first his shock of white hair, his scowl and an odd, deep scar in his forehead just scared the hell out of me, as it must have done to more than a few of the tourists.

The boys' dorm had one bathroom and one shower on each of two floors, neither of them copied from Vanity Fair or even the Lancaster Fair. I cringed when I stepped into the shower for the first time. It contained broken glass from a beer bottle. Life lesson learned: Do not bring glass into a shower, but do keep the beer cold by placing it in the toilet's water tank. We had no fridge.

The boys I met those first days were nice enough, though we would all learn a little later that two of the older ones, a couple of pals named Jack and Harvey, were bad actors who would try to get the rest of us into their troubles, without much success. They reminded me of the bad boys who got Pinocchio to run away. They didn't last the summer.

After inspectors from the Maine Central Railroad, which ran freight trains through Crawford Notch, came around to inquire about two missing, and important, signal lamps, Jack and Harvey left. I have no doubt a future life of crime lay before them or, at the very least, terms in the U.S. Congress.

A friend once told me that it was true that the Cog made those who stayed there stronger. Those who weren't up to the life quit after a few weeks or didn't come back a second year. But he said that the kinds of individuals who stayed to become Coggers, whether for two or three summers or for a lifetime, also gave much to the Cog and helped make the Cog the special place that it was.

Other kids working my first summer were a mix of big city teenagers (mostly from Philadelphia where the Teagues lived in the winter); southern college kids, the source of labor that had worked for Henry Teague and was still working for Arthur; and small-town boys like myself. At least one, I found out later, was the son of a commanding officer from Art Teague's regiment.

One of the local kids my first year would die the next at an Army camp, training for the Vietnam War. Another would bleach his hair completely blond, try to use a hammer and nail to relieve a badly blistered toenail, and was last seen, by me at least, running across the interstate in Concord. He said the police were after him.

Another local, Charley Kenison, would become general manager and oversee the Cog's transformation from steam to diesel.

I made no friends the first week or so, perhaps because I was homesick and had decided to get a letter to my dad to come rescue me. I had already begun the letter when I received one from my oldest sister. Much older, and wiser, than I, she wrote that my two other sisters, both closer in age to me, had already bet that I wouldn't last a week. That did it. I never looked back.

Not that the first summer was glorious. My years of experience watching my Lionel toy trains running around a track in the attic were ignored. I was put to work behind the lunch counter with the girls. When not doing that, I washed dishes and did kitchen cleanup. All of this for the magnificent sum of 80 cents an hour.

I wasn't pleased, but the girls were pretty. I began making friends at the dorm, and unlike the track and engine crews, I got one day off every week, which really began the love affair with the mountain and the Cog.

Chuck Berguido was my first Cog friend and one of the first kids from a big city that I came to know. He was one of the Philly kids, although not a friend of any of the Teague siblings. He was living at the boys' dorm and was a brakeman. It think it was his first year at the Cog, too, but he seemed quite sure of himself, and I hung on his every word.

He was a huge Bob Dylan fan, back in the day when Dylan was just gaining national prominence. I wish I was aware at the time that my dad's own best friend from younger summer days, John Hammond, was the Columbia Records impresario who first signed Dylan. Chuck would have thought that very cool. He seemed to hang on every lyric that Dylan had written and had memorized every stanza of "Tambourine Man."

Chuck had a chip on his shoulder. His father, he said, had been a vice president with Pan American Airlines, but his early death and the family's Hispanic name, he implied, had moved the family from well off to struggling. When I finally met his mother at the end of that summer, Col. Teague had brought her to our table to meet my father and mother.

Chuck noted that to me after lunch. Why hadn't it been the other way around? he asked. Perhaps, I thought, because there were several of us and just his mom at her table.

Chuck taught himself harmonica and guitar that summer. He offered to teach me, but I wasn't any good. Instead, I asked him to teach me to be a brakeman. Once a week, on my day off, I would trade in my lunch counter khakis and apron for a pair of dungarees and spend the day riding up and down the mountain with Chuck. That usually meant three trips, each lasting close to three hours.

It meant sitting outside on the front of the wooden passenger car on the way up, talking about anything and everything with Chuck, watching the cinders fall on us if the wind was blowing that way (you could actually hear the cinders hitting your clothes), and listening to Chuck give his speech to the passengers at Waumbek, the first of Arthur Teague's switches one-third of the way up the mountain.

We ate our lunches ("track lunches," itself a cool term, as was the "mystery meat" often included) either on the way up the second trip or at the summit hotel, which the greasy and grimy trainmen were encouraged to enter by way of a set of wooden steps that led directly to a wide kitchen window. Traipsing through the hotel's main floor was discouraged.

On one of those early trips, as I heard the cinders crunch while walking the few yards from the train to the summit hotel window and again smelled the coal, it occurred to me that I had been here before. This was not my mother's memory of her parents, this was mine. And it was correct. Our family had taken the Cog and stayed overnight in the Summit House hotel when I was about six years old.

The dimly-lit corridor, the feel of the rough hotel sheets, the sound of the wind rattling the windows, came back to me.

Now I was taking that train multiple times, listening to Chuck's speeches and gradually learning the routine from him and the other train crews, sweeping out the car between trips, washing the windows and soaping the exterior with a long-handled brush.

Each crew consisted of three: engineer, fireman, brakeman. And, yes, back then, it was all male, all the time. It would be a few years after my time at the Cog that female crew members were introduced. Even, shockingly, female engineers!

The crew census seemed to break down this way: There were always two or three older, grizzled engineers, plus two or three school teachers earning money on their summer breaks, and one or two younger ones, usually college students. Almost all had come up through the brakeman-fireman ranks, and most of them understood that while the tourists thought of this as just an amusing summer excursion, it was in fact serious business with serious consequences.

The engineer had the unchanging job, both going up and down, and the most responsibility. He had to check on the engine's condition, looking for loose or worn gears and pistons. He had to watch to make sure there was enough water in the boiler. He had to know his train's schedule and make sure his crew was prepared.

The fireman had the hardest physical work. On the way up, he shoveled a ton of coal on each trip, constantly scooping it up from the tender and then turning back to the firebox door, opening it with one gloved hand and in one motion tossing the shovelful of coal into the roaring flames.

I can still feel the heat on my face from peering inside to see how the fire was burning. I can still hear the slam of the fire door, which you always shut as fast as you could to keep in the heat.

For his reward, the fireman could rest on the way down. Some claimed they could even sleep.

The brakeman's work was intermittent and mostly light-hearted on the way up, but deadly serious on the way down. I have often thought that if Ma and Pa Tourist had fully understood that they were entrusting their lives and their kids to the sole charge of a 16-year-old boy on the way down the highest mountain in Northeastern America, the Cog Railway would have had far fewer paying passengers. Perhaps some passengers actually thought that way, but by the time they realized it, it was way too late to jump off and ask for a refund.

When I got there, the price of an adult ticket was $4.95. Years later, it would reach $60.

Chuck Berguido didn't address much that was serious in his speech, although he did point out that the steepness of Jacob's Ladder and the Long Trestle meant that passengers seated in the front of the car would be at those points some 20 feet higher than those in the rear.

And he might have casually mentioned that, on the descent, he would be using the two handbrakes outside the car's rear door to "keep the weight of the car" off the engine. Which meant, in fact, that this skinny kid from Philadelphia would be playing with two brake wheels that tightened or loosened two chains that ran beneath the car to asbestos-lined brake shoes that gripped either of the car's two axles. This would happen repeatedly on those two steep trestles, at Cold Spring Hill, and at many other points along the route.

On the way up, the brakes weren't used. The clang-clang of a metal ratchet, bouncing off the teeth of the cog wheel on the car, and a similar one on the engine, signaled that all was safe. The engine's power pulled itself up the track, which was bisected by a spooled cog rack, and the rack meshed with the cog wheel's teeth. The engine pushed the car. Simple.

If for some reason the engine failed, it would fall back onto its ratchet and the car would do likewise.

Aside from the speech, and the ticket collecting, which Chuck and other brakemen liked to do on a particularly steep part of the ride, the brakeman's duty on the way up was to throw the switch at the Waumbek water tank. The upgoing train would then move to the siding, allowing the downcoming train to pass. The ascending train would also take on water. It took 1,000 gallons for a single trip.

In my time, Larry Bowen was one of the fastest switch-throwers. And since the "most complicated switches in the world," have now been modernized, there is no one to challenge him. Bowen was one of three classmates from the elite Stony Brook prep school on Long Island who worked together at the Cog. It was the kind of connection that would repeat itself over and over. One teen would get a Cog job and then tell his friends back at school (high school or college). The next year, if the Teagues approved, the friends would join the first. It was part of the pipeline that fed the Cog a steady and fairly reliable work force.

For my third summer, I recruited a couple of teenage friends who had worked part-time with me at the Union Leader sports desk. One would come, and would eventually work there longer than I. The other backed out at the last minute, saying his father didn't want him to be away for the summer. It's too bad. Kevin O'Leary would become our high school class president and, briefly, a city cop. But he also became an alcoholic and died young. If he had come to the Cog, I'd like to think, things might have turned out better for him.

People would watch in awe as Larry Bowen maneuvered and danced his way through the complicated Cog switches. Because of the middle cog rack, moving the trains on and off a siding was no easy feat. Before Art Teague designed the switches, there were no up and down trains meeting and passing. There was no way to move one out of the way for the other to pass. Instead, trains would stop at one of two platforms along the way and passengers would have to switch cars.

Teague's switch consisted of nine moving parts, all of which had to be thrown by hand: five rails, two flags, and two cog racks with pins. And "a board," according to some brakemen's speeches. Over time, enough play had developed between the two tracks that a small board had to be wedged in as well.

One brakeman could easily handle the switching operation, given a little time. But some engineers, eager to keep their steam up and stay on schedule, didn't like to wait once they had backed off the switch and were again headed up the mountain. And it was a matter of some pride for the brakemen not to let that happen.

Once the down train had departed and his own train backed off the Waumbek switch, a good brakeman would step lively to lift and heave the heaviest rails into place, grab the greasy cog rack and pin it into place, throw the two flag handles, and almost instantly signal the engineer that he could come ahead. Some engineers didn't wait at all.

It was also a bit of a show for the passengers seated in the front of the car. You could feel their eyes on you as you ran through the steps, pretending to be nonchalant about it all. This sometime caused slips and banged knuckles and, rarely, a sliced finger caught beneath a heavy rail. Feet were well-protected in engineer's steel-toed boots, purchased either from a peddler who stopped by the Base Station once or twice a season or from Lahout's General Store in Littleton.

There was always some debate about the steel-toed boots. Critics argued that a steel reinforcement caught just right under a heavy falling weight could itself slice off one's toes. No one, though, had ever seen that happen.

The speech given by the brakeman usually came at Waumbek station, which the upcoming train would reach a few minutes in advance of the downcoming one. At the summit, the brakeman's job was to check in with the base ticket office by means of the direct phone line that ran beneath the tracks up the mountain. He needed to find out how many trains his would be meeting on the way back down and whether they were on schedule. The voice in the ticket office, invariably Cliff Kenney's, would bark "You're meeting one and one. Leave in 10 minutes" meaning you would meet one train at the Skyline switch and a second at Waumbek.

The brakeman would then make an announcement over the hotel PA system to the tourists and ring a bell and then make sure all were aboard who wanted to take the same train back down. Unless it was the final train of the day, people were given the option of staying longer at the summit.

The brakeman's real work was then about to begin. First was pushing off from the summit. This usually was no problem, as the engineer would have stopped the train so that it was still on a slight angle at the top. The brakeman might have to lean against the heavy car to get rolling and then hop on board.

But if the train was on the level at the top, which was always so if yours was the first end of a double-header (two trains), then a loop of chain would be tossed over a hook on the front of the engine and a wooden block on the car. Taking the chain off was always a delicate act. So was braking.

Braking was done by means of the two brake wheels roughly the diameter of a car's steering wheel. On the steepest sections, you would take up several notches of the chain by turning the brake wheel and then setting that brake by kicking a metal piece (the "dog") into a smaller toothed wheel at its base. You then moved quickly to take up slack on the second brake, playing that one while watching that you didn't "pull off" or did so just barely. Taking up too much on the second brake could have you pulling the car too far from the engine, leaving you to have to gingerly ease off on that brake to get back in place without smashing into the engine.

Mastering the brakes was a combination of sound, of feel, by location, and by the sight of the vapor plume coming from the engine's air valve. Shut down completely, the valve prevented air from leaving the cylinders, thus slowing the engine. Opened up, the engine sped up. Very simple.

Less simple, at least to me, was trying to figure out what that vapor plume was doing. I never did get it, though I swore to Chuck and to various engineers that I did. The first trip that Chuck let me brake was with a nasty little man named Gordon Chase, who cared for nothing and no one but Gordon Chase. In 1967 Chase would be the engineer in charge of an overloaded train that would derail at Skyline switch, killing eight passengers.

At the end of my first braking excursion, I confidently approached the engine to ask Chase how I had done (which was pretty good, I thought). I was rudely awakened. I told Chase I had carefully watched the air valve and adjusted it accordingly throughout the trip. He looked at me with disgust, then spat, swore and told me that this was all very interesting, but he had had to keep the "fuckin valve closed tight since Waumbek!"

Specific locations on the mountain had a lot to do with the art of braking. There were the obvious ones where the brakes needed firm application and attention, such as Long Trestle and Jacob's Ladder. There were the less so, like the Monkey Tree, a funny little tree that was halfway down Cold Spring Hill, the last steep descent before the Base Station. I think the Monkey Tree may have been a sassafras tree.

There was the cow pasture high up the mountain, just below the summit. There was Halfway House, a small shack painted red with white trim that had been put up not only to show the distance traveled but to astonish the passengers by its sign noting that the house was level despite looking as if it were lopsided. It had also been where passengers were transferred to another train in the days before Art Teague's switches.

For sound, the brakeman had the engine itself. Fifty years on, I can still hear the compressed air pushing through the cylinders and hear the engine's nuts and bolts shaking to get loose. That was also part of the feel. The engine shook violently at certain speeds, settled down at others. That is how I finally figured out how and when to apply the brakes. It was by feeling the engine and car through my feet and hands, and by listening.

When I did have it figured out, the work was mostly fun. The noise, the beauty of the nearest mountains and those across the far-off valleys below, were something that a relative handful of boys and men (and a few girls) have ever been lucky enough to experience in that way.

But before I had it figured out, it was terrifying. Not so much the thought of being cursed at by Gordie Chase. He was a prick; the other engineers were much more forgiving. But the idea that I was alone on this platform, responsible for the lives of men, women and little kids who were sitting right behind me, thinking they were in good hands, was sobering and scary. I was never so happy as when, after a few jittery days, or maybe it was weeks, I had it figured out. I was "qualified."

What I could not figure out, at least at the time, was people like Chase, or Frank Thompson, or some of the other rough older men who worked at the Cog. One winter, when I was still intending to go back to the railway for one more summer, I got a call at the newspaper from, of all people, Gordon Chase. He was working in Manchester for the winter, firing a boiler in some hotel. He was short of cash. Could I help him out?

For some reason, I said yes. He was just down the block, having called from a phone booth. I went down and found him standing in a doorway. He looked, as always, like a grubby, dark-faced rat in clothes. I gave him maybe $20 and sent him on his way. I don't believe I ever saw him again. Looking back, I'm sure that Chase was among those whom Art Teague had helped along through rough winters.

Firing

Even today, if I see a pair of workmen's gloves, I think of firing the Great Gulf, the number 6 engine and the easiest of all the engines to fire.

I don't remember exactly how I learned to fire or from whom. Mike Claypool fired for Griff Harris, one of the school teachers, when I was his brakeman on the Base Station. Mike probably helped. And I know Fred Kent helped me. He was firemen for Bob Kent (no relation) on the Ammonoosuc when I was a full-fledged brakeman. I'm guessing I pestered Fred to show me around.

I must have spent some time in the cab with these guys, sitting on the firemen's bench as they did their work. None were more than a year or two older than I. I still remember the heat from the firebox as the fireman opened and closed the door for what seemed to be a thousand times on a trip up the mountain.

The firebox door opened to the right, shielding the engineer from the intense heat. So if you were an apprentice fireman, or even just some special guest, sitting on the fireman's seat meant getting a very warm leg, even if you tried tucking it under your butt.

The fireman himself didn't feel the heat as much. He had those big work-men's gloves for one thing. He felt the heat the most on his face as he took quick glances into the firebox to make sure the coal was being consumed evenly by the flames. That was the secret to a good fire. Keep the fire burn-ing evenly. It even had a name. "Firing the corners," meant left, right, front and back. The coal would bounce back off those corners and, if you did it right, spread out fairly well.

If it didn't, there was always the hook, a long iron pole curved at the business end and with a handle at the other. It hung horizontally on the fireman's side of the tender. If the burning coal needed redistribution, or if a clinker was forming on the grate, you took the hook, opened the fire door, and vigorously and as fast as you could, put it in and dragged it back toward you. You could also apply the shaker bar, which actually opened the grate. It was a good way to knock out a clinker, but if you overdid it, you could lose half your fire dropping straight down to the ash bin below and possibly starting a fire on the tracks.

Whatever you did, you wanted to be quick about it because the longer the door was open, the more heat escaped and the more the steam pressure would drop, which elicited a corresponding rise in the temperature of the engineer, who was watching all this from his seat.

Firing was all about repetition. Turn to the tender, push your broad-faced shovel into the coal at the bottom of the pile, turn back to the firebox. Lift the handle on the firebox door with one gloved hand and swing it open. Toss in the load with the left hand nearest the coal on the shovel, now joined by the right hand, which would flip the shovel face down, spreading the coal to the hungry flames.

As you made these artistic moves, your eyes were constantly taking a quick mental picture, looking for how the fire was burning in the corners and what spot would get your next shovelful. You looked for holes where the fire had consumed the coal almost down to the grates below it. You would glance out the small front side window at the smokestack. What you wanted to see there was rich, thick black smoke. It meant you had a good fire burning.

You would also look at the steam pressure gauge. Each engine ran best at a certain psi, usually something a few pounds below pop-off pressure, which triggered an automatic release of steam.

Popping off was to be avoided as it brought down the pressure farther than you wanted. The 6 engine ran on so little steam that, early in my firing career, I was amazed (and thankful) that it was still chugging away with just 60 pounds of steam (pop-off was 120). I was thereafter called the "60-pound Duck" by one of the engineers.

Several things bothered firemen besides popping off or having an ill-burning fire. Falling arch bricks, plugged flues, fallen grates, those clinkers and lousy coal among them.

The arch brick was installed in the firebox of each engine at the beginning of the season. Made of a heavy material, it was designed to reflect the heat of the fire and thus raise the temperature in the firebox. It worked both in theory and reality, but the arch brick rarely lasted more than the first half of the season before the shaking of the engine caused it to fall. When it fell, it was invariably during a run up the mountain, and it was guaranteed to knock the hell out of your roaring fire.

Replacing an arch brick was a delicate and time-consuming job down at the shop. It meant the engine was out of service for at least a day, and that was money lost unless the spare engine was in working order. Even if it was, the spare was always the crappiest engine, the worst to fire and usually with a piece or two missing or about to fall off.

Plugged flues were worse than a missing arch brick. The flues ran front to back inside the engine structure, opening into the firebox and distributing its heat along the boiler to turn water into steam power. The flues would get plugged with coal dust over the summer and eventually had to be blown clean with a portable air pump apparatus.

Clinkers and lousy coal were often one in the same in that lousy coal didn't burn well, causing coal to turn into misshapen rock-hard pieces that would get stuck in the grates, making it impossible to shake down the fire and again requiring the hook's appearance.

Poor coal was the worst, though, making life miserable for the fireman and the engineer.

I suspect that Art Teague didn't always have the money for the best soft coal, which came from West Virginia and Pennsylvania mines.

Even with the Great Gulf, which was considered the Cadillac of the line and the easiest to get up the mountain with the lowest steam pressure, bad coal was no good.

The summer I fired it, the engineer was Bud Nye, who became a physician and cardiac surgeon. We got a particularly crummy run of coal for a week or so, and the heat between Bud and me could have produced steam all by itself. Try as I might, the stuff just wouldn't burn. At one point, with Bud nagging me to do better and me telling him what he could do with himself and the coal, he grabbed me with both hands, lifting me up to do God-knows-what as he sat in the engineer's seat. But I had hooked both my steel-toed boots under the seat's step, which made him all the angrier.

Somehow, we made it up the mountain.

It happens at some point to all crews over the course of a summer. When I became an engineer and Gordon Champion was doing the firing for me and lousy coal struck, I decided to show him the error of his ways. I ordered him into the engineer's seat while I showed him how to fire. After about 10 minutes of this, and having lost at least 10 pounds of our dwindling steam pressure, I handed him his shovel and said, "There! That's how to do it!" He didn't seem amused.

If they wished, the fireman and engineer had the culinary advantage of using the shovel, during a break between trips, to heat up a cheese sandwich or the "mystery meat" variety.

The fireman was also responsible for the fire at the end of the day. No one wanted to start a fire in a steam engine from scratch. It was a long process. Instead, the fire would be banked.

Banking meant letting the fire burn down on one side of the firebox and then adding several shovelfuls of coal on the other side, effectively burying the fire beneath a mound of coal. Only once or twice a summer would a well-banked fire flare up, usually when a strong wind blew off the mountain and raced down the line of engines, finding its way into the ash box and then up into the firebox.

One especially windy night found several of us firemen and engineers, roused from our sleep by the wind or an engine popping off, driving madly up from the boarding house to check on the engines. You kept the firebox door propped open overnight, usually with the heavy shaker bar, and on this night, the wind was blowing tongues of flame horizontally right out of the firebox and halfway across the cab. The sight was something out of Dante's "Inferno."

The Teagues provided room and board, of which Col. Teague gently reminded me when, after just my first few weeks of my first summer, I discovered I was earning about 80 cents an hour. (Seasonal employment in the tourist trade then and now is exempt from minimum wage laws.)

Not yet having fallen in love with the Cog, I sought out the colonel at the first opportunity and told him that I could be making more back at the new golf course next to my house then at his railroad as a counter boy/dishwasher. (Technically, I could have made more, if the golf course was still hiring laborers, which it wasn't.)

I'm not sure whether Art Teague was bemused or merely amused by this punk kid telling him about the economic facts of life, or whether he valued my father and the newspaper's influence. Judging from what I now know of him, I suspect he got a kick out of my temerity. In any event, having pointed out the room and board, the colonel nonetheless promised to think further on the matter. A few days later, I received a 10-cent raise. It helped with the laundry bill.

Room and board consisted of just that. A room, showers, and three squares a day. Bacon and eggs or French toast for breakfast, track lunches, and pretty good hot dinners from Pete, the cook, at the long kitchen tables each evening.

Recreation was whatever one could find to amuse oneself in the few off hours that weren't for sleeping. That might mean sitting around an outdoor fire in the evening while the girls sang or, if you were invited by one of the Teague daughters, a bridge game at the Hut.

Once a week, if you managed it, you caught a ride into Littleton, some 30 minutes away, to go to the Profile Laundromat to wash your clothes. While you waited, you could go for a pizza nearby or shop for work gear at Lahout's country store, which is where I bought my first denim work shirts and a pair of engineer boots. And met Joe and Gladys Lahout. Gladys was a buxom broad and a big hugger. Brother Joe seemed amused by how she squeezed the breath out of the Cog boys.

That first year, without my own car, I was dependent on others to get to Littleton. A few times, it was in one of the company-owned vehicles, including something called the Green Hornet, an old Chevy station wagon with a standard transmission whose shift was mounted on the steering axle. A French exchange student would drive.

One night, a few summers later when I had my own car, I made it all the way to and from Littleton and then realized I had forgotten my clean laundry. I think I set a land speed record for the journey back to town, slowing just before passing the State Police Troop F office. My laundry was where I had left it, folded on a side table at the laundromat. Why I was surprised that no one had absconded with it, I do not know.

By the end of my first summer, I knew I wanted to go back to the Cog again and again. At the start of the second summer, I could hardly wait for high school to end so I could get up to the Cog. By the third, I happily skipped out early from a high school graduation party in order to get on the road to the Cog. It had become a comfortable place, a place where I spent my teenaged years with friends, where we heard the Beatles on the car radio or in the boarding house after work, changing and evolving just as we were.

Friends

I had met girls at the Cog, too. But I had also awakened to them back home, particularly one from a neighboring town whom I would sometimes drive to high school. In fact, in my second Cog summer, she was also working away from home, at a resort on Lake Winnipesaukee, an hour's drive from the Cog.

On a rare day off, my buddy Joe Long and I drove down to see "my girl." We stopped for the night at my uncle's house in Holderness and then met Tina near the lake. Only Tina was anything but warm and friendly. When she told me she had met another boy, I was downcast. When she told me who it was, I was destroyed. It turned out to be one of my first-year Cog friends, who had not come back to the Cog. Instead he was working for his father at the lake.

There wasn't a lot of free time for dating or fooling around at the Cog, although some managed better than I. When we were on the train crews, glimpses were fleeting. And after work, if we managed to get up the strength to walk to the girls' dorm (a converted building that had once housed Old Peppersass), it was usually to nurse a beer, smoke a cigarette, and brag to the girls.

I was variously enthralled with "Fanny" Teague, one of Arthur's daughters; Sharon Riff, whose family owned a flower shop in nearby Lancaster; Linda "Heartless" Hartmann, who would marry a fellow Cogger; and Claire "the Bear" Dwyer, who was the company secretary and who used to wave to me from her office window at the start of each trip.

"Fanny" was the family's name for Frances Stratton Teague. But the others were nicknames of my own creation. I was into nicknames, I think, because my father and the owner of his newspaper were famous for applying names to political figures, i.e., "Dopey" Dwight Eisenhower, "Midnight" Harry Spanos, and the "Field Marshall" Marshal Cobleigh. Even all these years later, my friends refer to Claire the Bear, "Tricky Dick" Tirrell, and Jim "the Ape" McLaughlin, who served one year as brakeman for Frank Thompson.

Frank didn't have a nickname, but he came up with mine, which started as "McDuck" from the Donald Duck cartoons but soon shortened into just "Duck" (or the previously referenced "60-pound Duck"). Somehow, that name followed me back to Manchester and was used by friends at the newspaper. One pal there said I had better not get drafted because if ever told in a combat situation to "duck!" I was apt to look up to see who was calling me.

Chapter 4

CHARACTERS

Frank Thompson (center) and Gordon Chase (right) were neither teachers nor college students but they ran engines for Art Teague. At left is George Skrzypek.

CRAWFORD HASSEN CLAIMED to be related to Ellen Crawford Teague, herself a distant relation to the Crawfords of pioneering fame.

Crawford was the winter watchman at the Cog as well as the summer maintainer of the water/electric generation pump. He had a silver police badge of dubious origin. He was a pretty accomplished oil painter of the realist school, self-taught, I thought. It was years later that Tim Lewis discovered that Crawford's father had been a painter and that his mother's maiden name was indeed (Mable) Crawford.

One of his larger paintings was of a forest fire. It hung in Marshfield House. Legend had it that the frightened bear running out of the painting's flames was a late-winter addition that Crawford, under the influence of something, decided to add. It looked good to me.

It takes a certain type of man to isolate himself for months at a stretch in the deep snows and quiet nights of winter in the White Mountains. One late winter, Crawford's sister and her husband and son decided to pay him a visit. The sister died in the effort, freezing to death while trying to hike in on the unplowed Base Road.

Crawford had a gruff voice and a scary demeanor with a shock of close-cropped steel gray hair and a glass eye. But he was polite to tourists if they spoke to him and he was well-read, as one might expect of someone who spent the greater part of six months each year isolated at the base camp.

When he was in his cups, which was seldom in the summers, he could be belligerent or funny. He tolerated for the most part the men and boys who lived above his first-floor accommodations in the boarding house. His quarters included a spacious kitchen that had once served the whole house. But when we all went crazy with a water fight one night, leaving showers running and watching water flow down the stairs, Crawford was furious and colorful.

"Shit, piss and corruption are flowing down into my kitchen!" he roared up the stairs.

It was enough to end the water fight.

When I had my car, I would take Crawford to Littleton, the nearest big town, on occasion. He knew the works of Nietzsche and Kierkegaard, among others. He once loaned me a long and rambling disquisition he had penned. It was to me unreadable, but I am pained to this day that I never got it back to him. I think I didn't want to hurt his feelings.

Crawford loved the teenaged girls who worked at the restaurant and gift shop, and they fawned over him. He was particularly kind to little Lucy Teague, youngest of the Teague daughters and an often lonely girl. I have no idea how he came to be at the railroad, but Dale Granger, whose family had long ties to the Cog, was a longtime friend and pen pal of Crawford. She told Tim Lewis that Crawford said he had worked with the Blackfeet Indians out west.

Emile Rouleau spoke very little English. Actually, his English may have been quite good. He just didn't say much, in any language, and mumbled so that when he did speak, few could understand him.

Some people thought he was French Canadian, but I believe he was a Belgian and not a fan of the French. Legend had it that he went to Berlin, N.H. (at the time a big and boisterous French Canadian lumber city; it is now much smaller), got drunk and stood on a table in a French-dominated saloon to propose this toast:

"Here's to the Frenchmen. They're quite a race. They talk with their hands. And fuck with their face."

He was pummeled for that bit of verse and briefly held in the town drunk tank. He was one of many old-time Coggers whom Art Teague looked after and occasionally bailed out of jail.

Rouleau did odd jobs around the base camp. But many years before, when the hurricane of 1938 had devastated New England like no other before or since, he used his oxen team to bring in the logs with which the Marshfield restaurant and shop were built and with it two fieldstone fireplaces said to be among the largest in New England.

Bud Nye remembers trying to "keep up with old, frail Rouleau during my second summer when I was the coal bunker tender, gas station agent, honey wagon hauler and everything else while trying to get in a run as substitute brake man. We were issued scythes and told to cut the grass in the parking lot. I lasted about 10 minutes, stopping in agony. Rouleau continued cutting for the rest of the day."

Harold Adams, engineer's cap always pitched back on his head, a pipe clenched in his teeth, was a scary figure to those young train crew members who crossed his path at the engine shop. Those who worked hard, especially in the shop, could win Harold's respect, sort of. But if you stepped out of line, you might feel a pinch from one of his massive hands.

More than one young train man had seen the power of those hands and arms. The story was always the same: Two relatively strong young men would be attempting to lug or roll a tender or train wheel from one spot to another when "Old Weird Harold" would come along.

"What are you ladies doing?" he would say and then pick up the wheel, seemingly without effort, and walk away with it. In one telling, it was two of these massive wheels.

The shop men, some veteran boilermakers from the Boston and Maine, would test young college men who might think they knew it all. Bud Nye remembers Harold would hand a newbie a Styrofoam cup and instruct him to fill it from the kerosene pump to get the stove fire started.

"Of course, no matter how fast you ran, the cup dissolved before you reached the stove. Most of us did an about-face at this point and went back for reassignment to another location."

But, Bud added, the shop men could also be kind, helping him machine small parts for his Austin Healey sports car.

It was hard to tell how old were Harold and other long-serving members of Art Teague's crew. I was just a teen, so they all looked old and weathered to me. But apparently the hard life of the North Country had aged these men far beyond their chronological years.

Engineer Frank Thompson, for instance, looked to me to be at least in his 60s when I was there. When he died, friends who saw his obituary were stunned to see that he was 45 or 47 (the age varied depending on who was reading). At a reunion years later, several of us decided there was such a thing as "Cog years," not unlike dog years. The ratio was said to be 5 or 6 real years for every Cog year.

Frank had young crew members guessing about more than his age. There was great debate as to how many wives and children he had. Several times each summer, an old convertible or station wagon would pull to a halt at the Base Station and kids of various sizes and shapes would spill out and run up to him with shrieks of "Daddy!"

Frank was always polite but sometimes seemed puzzled as to which kid was which. But Frank was always good to his mother. So much so, that when she would die (this happened without fail at least once each summer when Frank needed a break from the trains), he would ask Col. Teague for time off for his mama's funeral.

I suspect Art Teague knew about Frank's mother's condition and the names of the Thompson kids, too. But if Teague or anyone knew to what summit location Frank would disappear on just about every trip, it was never divulged.

Frank's crews never knew. The fireman or brakeman would take Frank's order for a purple or brown "cow," a milkshake, hand it to him, and then Frank was gone, only reappearing when the passengers had been re-boarded and it was time to descend. One former fireman speculated that perhaps Frank had yet another wife stashed in a room at the Summit House. It is not beyond belief.

Larry "Father Goody" Gooden ran the track crew in the years I was at the Cog. I did not know much about him. The men and boys who worked on his crew were devoted to him and would quote, with great specificity, his instructions as to how a stringer or tie was to be placed in track repair.

His directions invariably began with a phrase such as, "By the red-blooded, bald-headed American Christ child..." followed by precise instructions. They were raunchy. But there was a basis for them in science. For instance, his directions to "knock a stringer up-mountain just one RCH" had their origin, whether Goody knew it or not, in World War II labs.

Working to refine the Norden Bombsite that would prove invaluable to American air forces over Europe before D-Day, engineers actually used a particularly fine female pubic hair of a particular color for the site's cross-hair. That bombsight no doubt saved Art Teague and thousands of soldiers in the field as it pulverized German defenses.

The track repairs went on endlessly as the mountain winds and weather, let alone the heavy cars and engines, wreaked regular havoc. Father Goody and crew would often take the first train up the mountain each morning and return on the last in the evening.

We would spot them along our own trips, usually sitting or standing trackside waiting for us to pass. Bud Nye says Goody would complain how his dog would chase him down the driveway every morning.

"One morning he stated he had solved the problem—he ran over his dog. I asked if the dog was OK and he said he would find out tonight when he got home."

Cog grease would play a role in a shameful incident involving Richard "Tricky Dick" Tirrell and one of the Roy brothers.

"Tricky Dick," so named by yours truly because it was the late 1960s and Richard M. Nixon was staging his comeback, was from Massachusetts. He was one of the odd kids out at the Cog. Shy and soft-spoken, Tricky had a mop of longish red hair that made him an easy target for some of the local folk who worked the Cog.

Putting Tricky on the track crew seemed a counter-intuitive move, but there wasn't a slot open on a train crew when Tricky arrived. How he got hired was a mystery to us at the time, but there he was. In fact, his mother had worked at a Massachusetts bank whose customers included a Mr. French of the Boston and Maine.

New and unknown to others in the boys' dorm, he was initially not invited along for Friday night laundry and pizza runs to Littleton. When we came home that first night after Tricky had been there a week or two, we discovered him cleaning his clothes in a wash basin in the bathroom. With a stick.

Quietly, we decided he could come with the gang next laundry day. But we couldn't do anything about Clayton Roy.

Clayton Roy was of a type of red-neck yahoo that will always be with us. Short and clearly suffering from short man's syndrome, Clayton was loud and strong, with muscles bulging from his tee shirts and a mean look in his eye.

Clayton worked on the track crew. That was a given. He could use track tools. Once in a while, he would be used as a fireman, but not often. It was as if the management knew that the guy was not the engineer type, so why bother wasting a fireman's spot.

His brother, Ernie, was the class act that Clayton was not. Ernie was second to Pete the Cook in the kitchen. He was quiet, with heavy glasses, and a pleasant demeanor. He reminded me of Mr. Peepers, the bookish character played on a 1950s TV series by Wally Cox.

He was also well-spoken and well-read. No surprise there. If you are in a family with the likes of Clayton Roy and you are bookish, you might as well make the most of it.

But there was more than met the eye with Ernie Roy. It was something I didn't believe myself until another Cogger pointed it out to me. Loudmouth Clayton was scared of quiet Ernie. And, it turned out, with good reason. Ernie, in his white tee shirt and apron and with his reserved ways, seemed small. But look close, my friend said. Ernie's muscles were not on display like Clayton's, but they were there and their owner brooked no nonsense from his asshole of a brother.

I saw them come nose to nose in the kitchen one morning over something. Clayton raised his voice. Ernie didn't raise his but quietly told his older brother to shut up. There were others around, so it must have pained Clayton even more, but after glaring at his brother for half a second, Clayton backed up and walked meekly out of the kitchen.

I wish Ernie had been on the track crew when Clayton went after Tricky Dick, but in the ensuing encounter, it really wasn't necessary. Clayton, the typical schoolyard bully, was on Tricky about his hair from the first day. The Beatles had brought longer hair into fashion, but fashion had not penetrated Clayton Roy's skull.

When Clayton harassed and goaded, Tricky was like the Tar Baby, saying nothing in return, only firing up Clayton more. Finally, Clayton couldn't take Tricky's Gandhi-like silence. He took a big daub of cog grease from a can and smeared it into Tricky's red locks. He no doubt expected Tricky to finally respond to that affront.

Nope. Tricky just went on about his business while Clayton wondered what could possibly provoke this fellow. Other track crew members stood around uncomfortably.

A footnote to the Tricky-Roy affair. Clayton Roy was not invited back the next year. Tricky, however, worked his way up from brakeman to engineer. He later took up residence in a Thoreau-like cabin in the Massachusetts woods, where he filled notebooks with his writing. Tricky Tirrell's dad won the Silver Star in the South Pacific. The son doesn't know if Col. Teague was aware of this connection.

While I didn't know Larry Gooden anywhere near as well as his track crew members did, I did see him cry once. It was on the way back to the Cog from some supply trip to Lancaster in one of the big old trucks the Cog kept. This one had a stick shift on the floor, and I was assigned to drive Goody. We took a shortcut, and Goody directed me to stop at the remains of a faint driveway from which one could make out the outline of a cellar hole, a common site in rural New Hampshire.

Goody got out, walked a ways down the driveway, and paused. Several minutes passed. When he got back into the truck cab with me, he pulled out a bandana and wiped his eyes and blew his nose.

As we drove the short distance back to the Cog, Goody explained that where we had stopped was where he had been born and raised and he was thinking of his mom and dad. He didn't have to say anything else. I felt proud to be his confidante, although surprised to see Old Father Goody moved to tears. Such shows of emotion were rare among the wizened old men who worked alongside young boys at the Cog. But I came to realize that the North Country men were not unlike others, down deep.

Turns out that Goody, like others among the older Coggers, had a winter job nearby. He was on the town road crew, plowing snow in the winter in his hometown of Carroll. (Carroll, like other New Hampshire places, was better known by the names of its three villages: Fabyans, Twin Mountain, and Bretton Woods. Groveton is similar. Few know that the incorporated name is Northumberland.)

I would see such a show of emotion only one other time from old, tough Coggers.

The day Art Teague took his life, I saw both Paul Philbrick and Jitney Lewis sit in the grass with tears welling up in their eyes. Jitney, perhaps the stronger of the two, would recover. Paul, it turned out, never did.

Pete and Grace Rusinski were the odd couple of the Cog. Pete claimed past military service (perhaps the Col. Teague connection?). His favorite lines included telling train crew members there was to be "no fraternizing" with his waitresses and counter girls, and as a season neared its end, he would say it was time to "get out the crying towel," as summer romances faced their inevitable end.

Pete's self-proclaimed favorite friend was "Uncle Bud," and if he ever drew a completely sober breath, I missed it. The smell of Listerine vied for top Pete scent along with stale Budweiser breath. A case of beer a day, which meant several trips to the "walk-in" cooler at the boarding house, was the average for Pete.

His standard uniform was stained white pants, stained white tee shirt, and an apron, which was stained. He was master of his domain, which was the kitchen that provided meals for the employees as well as for tourists at the snack bar or in the adjoining dining room. Pete's conversational repertoire consisted of "toot suite," "pdq" and "order up," and that "crying towel" business.

I know of several romances that outlasted not only winter separations but Cog years entirely. Marriages came directly out of some Cog summers. And others were sparked there but only became serious years after.

Pete was tall, over six feet, and broad. He would have to bend his head down to lean through the cluttered service counter to ask you what you would like for breakfast. (Standard fare of French toast, eggs over easy, bacon and the like.)

Pete was married to Grace. She was a little person or midget, but no one remarked on the fact or that about two feet of height separated her from her spouse.

They drove a big American station wagon, and the first time Grace told me to drive it somewhere, I knew how they could. It had the kind of electronic seat movement that is often standard these days but was rare back then. Grace could move the seat up several inches, in order to see over the dashboard, and forward so that her feet could touch the blocked pedals. It was, of course, an automatic transmission. Grace would have never been able to depress a clutch. As it was, the two drove the car to and from their winter jobs at Florida hotels.

Where Pete was easy-going for the most part, Grace was the no-nonsense mess sergeant Pete was said to have been. Someone had to be. Feeding hundreds of people a day, ordering tons of food (kept in a "walk-in" freezer at the side of the boarding house), and overseeing the waitresses and kitchen crew was a tough job.

Plus, Grace had to be on watch for the state health inspector.

It wasn't that we were surprised by an inspection visit. Whether by authorized arrangement or because someone always told someone in advance, Grace knew when a visit was to be made and her staff knew that work was ahead.

Grace had us clean everything imaginable from the customer counters to the soda and frappe machines to the utensils. And then she had us clean them all again.

She even made her mother, a wizened old thing resembling Mammy Yoakum on a bad day, keep her little dog out of Marshfield on inspection day.

"Ruthie" was Grace's mom. She cleaned the boarding house, not an easy job. She was harmless but no doubt shocked tourists as much as Crawford Hassen could. Her dog, nicknamed "Pig" out of earshot of Grace, pretty much pulled the tiny Ruthie around the Base Station on a leash. And in one celebrated instance, a well-placed slingshot slug hit the dog in its hind quarters, causing it to bolt out of the Marshfield double-doors. Alas, "Pig" went out the open side while Ruthie slammed into the closed door.

A second odd Cog couple, Archie McDonald and his common-law wife, were there for only my first year or two. Archie was part of the contingent of older engineers, similar to Frank Thompson and Gordon Chase, as opposed to the teaching contingent. One story had it that Archie, firing a trip for Chase, didn't take kindly to Chase berating him, so he threw the shovel into the fire and told Chase to fire for himself.

I had heard that Archie had once been an engineer for the B&M. His wife, we were told, was an American Indian, but no one I knew ever got close enough to speak with her. If looks could kill, a glance in a mirror would have been the end of Mrs. Archie.

Like most of the other spouses who lived at the base, she had a job. Hers was attendant at the ladies' room. She had few customers. She would station herself directly in front of the door and her scowl would drive most women, especially those with daughters in tow, to whisper "we will wait until we get to the top, dear."

John Weigel just appeared one day shortly after the Cog summer season had begun. Rumor had it that he was an MIT or Clemson grad with an engineering degree. I was later told that he in fact went to Dartmouth and the California Institute of Technology. It was difficult to tell how old Weigel was. I guessed he was north of 30, but using the "Cog years" measurement, he may have been only 22 or so.

Weigel slept in his car that summer. Slept there and pretty much lived in the Volkswagen Bug from which he had removed the front passenger seat, replacing it with his bed.

The rest of the interior was packed to its roof with his gear. The little kids at the Cog were fascinated by Weigel and his "home." He spoke with a high-pitched, scratchy voice, but he spoke little, preferring to have his nose in a book when he wasn't working.

Since he had come in later in the season, after the train crews had been made up, he was sometimes a spare fireman or brakeman, as well as putting his reputed engineering background to work in the shops.

Chapter 5

TROUBLE ON THE LINE

*Breakdown on the mountain might mean transferring passengers. Shop crew
Harold Adams (left) and Paul Philbrick (right) helped on this one.*

PERHAPS TWO OR THREE TIMES IN A SEASON, a mechanical breakdown would occur somewhere on the line. Despite a machine shop that could fix about any problem, and machinists who were careful and rightly proud of their work, engines that had been thumping and pounding up the mountain for decades would suffer fatigue.

Remarkably few of these incidents caused accidents, perhaps a testament to Arthur Teague and the men he had selected to work for him. Was he using some secret formula that, as with his war years, had allowed him to get the best out of a group of disparate individuals?

Word would reach the trains either at the summit, where a phone check to the base ticket office was required, or at the Skyline or Waumbek switches on the line.

The brakeman might be told to re-check in with the base at one of those switches. That meant pulling out the track phone, which each car carried as standard equipment. They were actually World War II surplus crank phones that Arthur Teague had acquired. Their leather cases still retained the faded "U.S. Army" stamp. I wonder how many times Col. Teague used ones just like them while fighting his way across the hedgerows of France.

Tim Lewis came across a Stars and Stripes Army newspaper column by Jimmy Cannon (later of New York newspaper fame) in which Col. Teague and a German commandant banter over the phone while trying to arrange the Germans' surrender.

At the Cog, a phone's alligator clips would be attached to the phone wires that ran beneath the tracks from base to summit. A crank handle would alert the ticket office at the base to pick up and the brakeman, or in some cases the engineer, would receive instructions.

On a cloudless July or August day high atop the Presidential Range, killing 20 minutes or half an hour while the problem below you was fixed wasn't such a bad thing. You did have to worry about the tourists, of course. Sometimes, you just told them they had to stay on board. Too dangerous to be walking around on uneven terrain, be it rocks or a railroad track smeared in cog grease and creosote.

But on other occasions, if your car was stopped on a fairly level spot (they have such things, even on a mountain), you could let the tourists out to stretch their legs and take pictures, and you could sit back, smoke a cigarette, and enjoy the view.

Not that the weather was always so pleasant. The mountain holds the world record for the highest land wind speed. Its fans proudly claim that Mt. Washington is home to the world's worst weather. No doubt there are other spots, but they are not regularly inhabited and thus have no organic rooting section.

The weather can turn in a minute, making us marvel when families would show up at the base and read the weather board that ticket master Cliff Kenny chalked up each morning and hung outside his window. A typical July day, sunny and 70 degrees at the base, would list the summit as "foggy, some rain, temperature 45."

The family might look up, see the clouds enveloping the mountain, and decide to hike up rather than ride the Cog. Outfitted in shorts, sneakers, and tee shirts, they would head off.

We could only shake our heads.

I could also hate the weather on occasion. Not long into my career as a brakeman, the weather turned foul. Here it was in early July, and the morning broke with rain, whipped around by wind with temperatures in the low 50s. I was sure no trains would be running. But going into the kitchen for breakfast, I was told otherwise.

I loaded my train, only half full, and up we went. It was a miserable trip sitting alone on the platform outside the wooden car. It was bad enough that I came close to wishing that I was in one of the two aluminum cars that Art Teague had had built a decade earlier.

To me, those bigger cars with their huge windows seemed out of place on our steam railroad. But on this trip, getting soaked and cold, I actually envied the brakemen on the Chumley and Thelma cars. They had no out-side decks, so the brakemen sat or stood in indoor comfort.

When I checked in with Cliff Kenny once we got to the summit that morning, he told me I would be meeting "one and one" on the way down, meaning one train at Skyline switch and another farther down at Waumbek.

I couldn't believe it. What idiots would pay to come out in such weather? And what was Col. Teague thinking to allow trains running in such dangerous conditions? Well, dangerous in my expert estimation. I was 17, and very cold.

Rain pelted me, and my fingers were nearly frozen on the descent. When we got down, after what seemed like hours, I was sure we would be told there would be no more trips that day. Wrong.

The weather, in fact, was improving. Tourists were showing up, and in a business that needed every fare every day in the short summer season, the colonel was going to have trains moving. I shook my head and went inside to pick up track lunches for my crew from Pete and Grace in the kitchen.

Still, I ended up being a very good brakeman. I would also be a compe-tent fireman. As for engineering, well, I was lucky.

I liked the brakeman's job because it was, for much of the time, solitary work. The fireman and engineer shared the cab for the entire trip. My inter-action was with the passengers, and it occurred at the beginning, halfway up (to give a speech), and at the end. The rest of the time, I was either sit-ting alone on the exposed front of the car or again by myself on the back braking platform, the passengers on the other side of the door behind me, the engineer and fireman in the cab ahead of me.

The ride up was spent looking at distant peaks or down at 100 years of cinders, cog grease, and lichen-covered rocks. The brutality and ferocity of the mountain hit me each time we passed the plain wooden monument to Lizzie Bourne, a hiker who had perished in a storm, less than a quarter of a mile from shelter at the summit.

The bright days had me marveling at the cow pasture, where 100 years before, hotel owners had kept cows all summer long to provide milk for Summit House guests.

I also spent much of one summer watching Ken Curran of Littleton, whom I would know later through state politics, go bankrupt in attempting to tear down two structures the U.S. Air Force had built in the 1950s, one to test jet engines and the other as a dormitory to house the testers.

To withstand the arctic-like conditions, and to properly test engines for B-52s that would be flying 24-7 to guard against the Soviets, the buildings were built to last. Last they did, finally succumbing to the wrecking balls only after more than a year of effort.

Forty years on, their square concrete bases can still be seen.

The U.S. military has also used the mountain's weather and geography as a testing ground for ground troops and helicopters. Army Ranger units would suddenly appear at the summit or base and the train crews would be told that the rangers were to ride for free. I wonder now how Arthur Teague may have interfaced with the Army forces. Did they even know of what he had done on a summer, 25 years earlier, with a real enemy all around him?

It wasn't just jet engines or Army rangers to which the mountain played host through the years. A pilot named Carmen Onofrio managed to land and take off from the summit in a small fixed-wing aircraft. Sikorsky himself tested his helicopters there. And for years before the Wright Brothers flew, the daily summer newspaper Among the Clouds recorded comings and goings on and around the mountain.

The newspaper had its own tiny print shop on the summit and an unusual method for some of its deliveries. It would use a slideboard, also known as a "Devil's shingle." The contraption had been built while the Cog track itself was under construction. Built for one rider, the small board fit snugly over the cog rack and was slowed by application of a hand brake.

Without the brake, speeds of more than 60 miles an hour were said to have been met. There were also age-old tales of workmen neglecting to remove a crowbar or other tool from the middle rack as a slideboarder came whistling down.

One tale had it that a rider once hit such an object doing more than the fabled 60 mph and was launched into the brush and tundra, never to be seen again.

Such tall tales weren't necessary. There were enough real accidents, including at least one fatality, to finally convince railroad management to ban the board, although some illicit rides were still taken on the remaining boards. One such was on display for tourists at Marshfield Station when I worked there.

❋

Despite six or seven-day work weeks, Coggers found time for fun. On the hottest days, a favorite spot was the Upper Falls of the Ammonoosuc. It was just a mile or two down the Base Road and offered shade, pretty scenery and various levels of swimming and diving. And it was all set to the background roar of the falls themselves, which made it tough to hear when you were close to them.

The two big attractions there were a huge, bowl-like pool into which the falls tumbled and roared, and a natural water slide, whose trough was worn remarkably smooth after who knows how many centuries.

You could ease yourself into the trough, let go, and be carried dozens of yards downward and then, whoosh, right over the side and into the bowl.

That was much less daring than diving or even jumping from the heights into the bowl pool itself. I must have jumped a time or two, but I know damned well that I never had the bravado to dive, as some did. There was a sizable space behind the waterfall. Coggers who had jumped or slid down the falls would duck into the space while others would alarm unsuspecting tourists by screaming that their buddy had not surfaced.

Other than laundry night in Littleton, occasional forays were made to a drive-in movie theater in Whitefield or a Saturday night trip to Newell's Dance Hall, a Forrest Lake spot in Whitefield. It was a favorite of teens and young adults in the area, attracting Bette Davis (who lived in nearby Sugar Hill) to dance to big bands in the 1930s and featuring the rock group called Aerosmith (also with New Hampshire ties) into the 1970s.

For us, it was a place to see some pretty new faces but the intermixing of Coggers with the locals could also make for some scenes out of a rural "West Side Story" with Sharks vs. Jets lining up on opposite sides of the dance floor. No fights broke out when I was there, but there were plenty of staredowns, sharp words and testosterone.

Litttleton was not just for pizza, supplies and laundry. It was the largest town nearby, and its hospital and other services had been regularly used by the Teagues and Coggers over the years. I found that out one evening when a fake fight I was engaged in with my Cog mate, Joe Long, went awry.

We would attempt to fool tourists (who probably weren't paying attention in any case) by staging fake fights and throwing our then-nimble bodies down stairs or hillocks. In one such effort, Joe accidentally came too close with a flying elbow. It caught me flush in the face, and when I spit out the blood, a couple of teeth came with it. Fanny Teague and her mom conferred, and it was decided I should go to see Littleton dentist Dr. Robert "Crow" Enderson. Fanny drove me to his house, it being after business hours.

Crow was obliging (I think he had an eye for Fanny) and agreed to examine me.

"Yes sirree, Champ," he said, "you need some work. We will have to go to my office."

I made a motion for the door, but Crow interceded.

"Not yet, Bub," he said. "The Packers and the Cowboys are on. You can wait 'til halftime, can't you? Would you like a cold beer? Oh, wait, that probably wouldn't be a good idea, with your teeth and all."

I thought he was kidding. Not only about serving beer to an underaged teen but also that we would be waiting until a break in a pre-season football game before I could get looked at.

He wasn't.

I learned through years of friendship that sports, football in particular, was important to Crow, his brother "Pepper," and even to his gorgeous wife, "Red."

So Crow showed me to a couch. We watched the game. And then he took me to his office and gave me temporary crowns, one gold and one silver, for my missing teeth.

"You look like a pirate, Hoss," he told me. And I did.

Luckily, my father stopped by for a visit the next day. He was flying around the state with the aeronautics director, a personal friend, and they had decided to stop by to see me. They flew me back to Manchester, and I had permanent caps in place within a few days. I took a bus from Manchester to Littleton and hitched my way back to the Cog.

That may have been the longest I ever spent away from the Cog during a summer season, except one trip to Hampton Beach with Mark Jordan, an erstwhile boyfriend of Fanny Teague (there were many), until my final summer.

That final year I drove to Philadelphia with Tom "Sticky" Baker to help move the Teagues up for the season. Sticky was a name he picked up for taking a light bulb from a police van to replace another one at a horse show. He would marry Margie Teague. "Tom and Margie" was pretty much one name for the entire time I was at the Cog. They had been going together forever. One year, they helped run the Summit House hotel.

It was at the hotel where Tom got the call the afternoon Art Teague ended his life. With the last train long gone, there was no easy way for Tom to get down to Margie and the family. A stage down the Auto Road would have meant a long ride around the mountain from Pinkham Notch.

Instead, accompanied by Nick Chaykowski, who worked at the hotel and later the Cog, Tom walked down the Cog tracks, with the last part of the journey in the dark.

There was not a lot of free time, but some of us managed to do some climbing. We had the Presidential peaks just sitting there every day. The two most direct trails to the summit of Mt. Washington started at the Base Station. The most popular and prettiest was the Ammonoosuc Ravine Trail, which wound its way up to trace Abel Crawford's bridle path and pass the Lakes of the Clouds before reaching the summit. After the Teagues sold the railway, there was controversy when the owners began charging a parking fee for use of a lot that hikers had always enjoyed for free.

The other trail, reached by crossing a small footbridge over the Ammy, was the Jewell. It was longer, had more of its length below tree line, and could be boring.

Several of us spiced things up after work one evening by trying to drive the Cog jeep up the Ammonoosuc Trail. The jeep was used for pulling the "honey bucket" to collect trash and garbage. It was nearby when we got the idea.

It wasn't successful. We managed to get it perhaps 200 feet up the trail before the woods closed in on it. It took a dozen of us several minutes of lifting and heaving to get the thing unstuck.

Cog Parties were held at the end of each summer season. Timed, I guess, to catch the most people before they were back to school, either as students or teachers, and before the fall season reduced the schedule of train trips, they were much anticipated.

In my first two years, with Arthur still there, these were marvelous times. I helped Tim Bemis one year with a song he was writing, set to the tune of the Kingston Trio's "Charlie on the MTA." Tim had cleverly worked in several of the current Cog engineers, complete with their proclivities or mannerisms or both. It included these stanzas:

"Well let me tell you a story of a man named Bobby (Bob Kent, engineer and school teacher) on that tragic and fateful day. Put some coal into his tender, kissed his wife and family, took a ride on the Cog Railway.

"Well did he ever return? No, he never returned. And his fate is still unlearned. He may ride forever 'neath the trestles of that mountain. He's the man who never returned.

"Well Bobby loaded his passengers at Marshfield station and headed up for the top. But when he got to Waumbek he met Gordie coming down and old Gordie just couldn't stop."

Refrain.

"Well right behind Gordie came old Frank Thompson like a bat out of hell, by heck. Took a look at the pileup, opened up his air valve, and flew right over the wreck.

"And right behind Bobby came a man named Jitney, Little Jesus with a will to save. Couldn't get around it so he smiled and gave a thumbs-up wave."

Interesting that the "Gordie" Chase of the song was already well known for his penchant for speed. That recklessness would make even worse the fatal accident that occurred two years after that song was sung, at the time to peals of laughter.

I have found few Coggers with whom Art Teague spoke of his war experiences. Like many veterans of that "greatest generation," he didn't see the need to relive what a lot of men like him had gone through. He, and they, were all about making a living, raising their families and trying to forget the hell of the recent past.

Looking back, I wonder at the war connections between Col. Teague and others of his generation who either worked with him at the post-war Cog or whose sons did.

I have mentioned my own father, intimately familiar with the territory that Teague crossed in Europe that summer, fall and winter after D-Day. And there was Gen. John Ruggles, who had commanded the 22nd before Teague and whose son, John, would work at the Cog. Gen. Ruggles and Art Teague stayed friends, and Ruggles would take a cabin at the Cog for a few weeks for several summers.

My engineer on the Great Gulf, Bud Nye, doesn't remember if he ever spoke with Col. Teague about his own father. But Col. Glenn Nye's 322nd Bomber Group, B-26 Marauders nicknamed "Nye's Annihilators," had flown many missions over Hitler's Europe in the two years leading up to D-Day.

They then gave Gen. Roosevelt and Col. Teague close-in bombing support on Utah Beach just before they landed on June 6, 1944.

Two southerners by birth (Glenn Nye was born in Shelby, North Carolina), did Cols. Teague and Nye know each other during the war? Did Col. Teague know that it was Nye's son he was hiring 20 years later?

Bud Nye was just six years old when his dad was killed in the next war, his B-26 bomber hit by enemy fire over North Korea and lost with four men aboard.

Yet another Cog-Teague-war connection: Jack Dwyer. His daughter, Claire, would serve as office secretary at the Cog during my years there.

Only later did she realize that her dad, a recipient of the Distinguished Flying Cross, had flown combat missions over the Normandy beaches on D-Day with the 351st Fighter Squadron.

In just 100 days that summer of 1944, Jack Dwyer flew his P-47 Thunderbolt on 71 missions. Did Dwyer fly alongside Glenn Nye's 8th Air Force bombers? Were the two pilots fighting the air war overhead while Art Teague was moving in from the beachheads below?

If Art Teague's nerves had been shaken by his war years, he didn't seem to show it.

Norm "Jitney" Lewis, longtime Teague friend and Cogger, remembered one incident involving a cook at the Summit House who had gone berserk and barricaded himself in a room, armed with a knife.

Reached by phone at the base, Arthur took a train to the summit, walked to the man's room and told the fellow he was either coming out immediately or Arthur Teague was coming in, and it wouldn't be pretty for the man if Arthur Teague came in. The man came out.

Art and Ellen worked long days and watched their family grow. Janie was followed in quick order by three pretty girls, Margie, Frances (Fanny) and Anne. A bit later came Lucy and finally Charlie.

Arthur dealt with fluctuating coal prices, the fickleness of summer help, and state bureaucrats, many of whom didn't like it that a private concern owned that right of way to the summit of the state's highest mountain, let alone a hotel at the top.

In lean years or not, Ellen Teague liked to entertain or visit other White Mountain attractions. They would dine at the Crawford House, watch plays at the Weathervane Theater and swim in the pool at the Mountain View Grand Hotel in Whitefield.

The Bretton Woods Boys Singers had a summer camp a few miles from the Cog base. The camp's owners were friends of the Teagues, and the boy singers would often come to entertain in the Marshfield House dining room and for special events.

The Teagues also owned a farm in Guildhall, Vermont, complete with a hired hand. He had the old Yankee first name "Carroll," and he reminded me then and now of the "Gus" character who gave avuncular advice to the title character on the "Leave it to Beaver" TV series.

The farm's fields ran right down to the Connecticut River, which divides Vermont from New Hampshire. (I like the fact that New Hampshire took the matter to court and was determined to own the river right up to the Vermont shoreline.) During haying season, some Coggers would be sent over to the Teague farm to help bring in the bales. I was one of them and not too fond of the chore. I had had my fill of haying back home.

But the hour-long ride in the back of a stake truck was cool on a hot summer day, and Col. Teague would treat us all to ice cream at a roadside stand on the return trip.

Several of the Teague girls owned show horses, and the family competed at fairs throughout New England. Even Mrs. Teague participated with horse and buggy. It was not inexpensive.

Just the twice-yearly commute between the Cog and their Philadelphia home was an economic and logistics undertaking. Art Teague had designed and helped build his home at the corner of Oak Street and Northwestern Avenue in posh Chestnut Hill. It was a handsome house, and Ellen kept up with Philly's Main Line society. Two of her daughters would have coming out parties there.

The moves back and forth from Philly to the Cog weren't easy on the Teague children. Margie and Fanny started the school year each fall in tiny Twin Mountain and then, after the Columbus Day close of the Cog, would re-enroll in Philadelphia.

Janie, it seemed, worked the hardest at the Cog, overseeing the dining and snack bar facilities and taking regular turns at the cash register. Whether it was the work or her Type 1 diabetes, she was rarely pleasant to any but a few close friends. Her parents, indulging her because of her disability, said little.

Jitney Lewis knew both Henry and Arthur, having come to work in 1950 as a friend of George Trask. Jitney had lived on a Vermont farm, which was good enough a resume for Henry. Jitney fired for legendary Mike Boyce, who was tough as nails but who bought Jitney an ice cream at the end of his first summer. Boyce had worked there about 40 years when Jitney first arrived. Boyce may have been the last to fire using wood.

Jitney worked well with Art. He said Art taught him how you were only as good as those who worked for you, and so Art tried to hire good men. But he also had a soft spot for his men and, in the winter, would occasionally help out someone down on his luck, financially or otherwise.

Jitney was once hit by lightning on the mountain. He was OK, and even though his bell had been rung, he accepted Art and Ellen's invitation to go out to dinner that evening. Jitney tells with pride that Art was a pretty big deal in New Hampshire's North Country, so when he called and asked the restaurant to remain open past closing time, it was done.

Jitney favored Manhattans. At dinner, a pitcher was produced at their table. After two or three of these, Jitney told Art that if this was the way he was to be treated in such circumstances, he would go up the mountain the following day, hoping to find another thunderstorm.

Jitney says Arthur did not speak to him of his war years. But he, too, considered Arthur an exceptionally brave man. Besides the crazed cook at the summit, Jitney recalled a huge windstorm that was ripping the roofing shingles from the top of the three-story men's boarding house.

Arthur and several employees climbed up on ladders, but while the others clung unmoving to the ridgepole, Arthur was calmly walking along the edge of the roof, inspecting and repairing as he went.

"That," Jitney heard someone say, "is the bravest man I have ever known."

Above: Art and Ellen
Teague in happy times
at a season-ending Cog
Party. (Elvira Murdoch/
Lewis Family)

Left: Tickets were slightly
cheaper in those days.

There were girls at the Cog
in the '60s but never on train
crews. Waitresses Sharon Riff,
Fran Conkey, and Carolyn
Poltrack worked at Marshfield.

Clockwise, from lower left: Jitney Lewis, Emile Rouleau, Harold Adams,
Larry Gooden, Crawford Hassen, and Steve Christy, Coggers all.

A double-header on Jacobs Ladder.

Henry Teague (seated at left) owed much to Dartmouth College. He was in its first Tuck Business School class. (Courtesy of Dartmouth College Library)

Families were a big part of the Cog. Engineer Bob Kent holds son, Jeff, in his Deuce cab.

Above and right: A great look down mountain from above Long Trestle and a look at a train ascending Jacobs Ladder.

Left: Owner Arthur Teague (white shirt) helping in a mid-mountain breakdown.

In 1938 a hurricane decimated the Cog and caused Henry Teague to get a loan from Dartmouth College.

Chapter 6

BAD SUMMER

Gov. John King (left) views Chumley car where eight passengers died in the worst accident in the Cog's history. (Union Leader file)

THE PROFIT MARGINS that the Cog ran on were pretty slim. Unlike today, where improvements to engine power and switches, and a longer season, have pushed passenger loads into the 90,000 plus per year, Art and Ellen Teague's numbers were much lower. A 45,000-passenger year was huge. And each time a record mark occurred during a season, Art provided a special bonus to all Coggers.

Even so, every nickel counted. Every bad-weather day, every breakdown cut into the profits.

The bad year of 1967, the one that would crush Arthur Teague and nearly destroy his family, had been foreshadowed at the end of the 1965 season, though no one could know it at the time.

The Hut, the big old comfortable log house that had been Henry Teague's home at the Base Station and had become home to Art and Ellen Teague and their family each season, had burned to the ground.

The cause was never determined. The Teagues vowed to rebuild, but they had to dig deep. Worse, they were storing Cog artifacts and memorabilia in the Hut in anticipation of the 100th anniversary of the railway in 1969.

The Hut was gone, a pile of sticks and ashes. Art and Ellen and their two youngest children would live the summers of 1966 and 1967 in one of the small cottages normally used by the married engineers and their families.

Rebuilding started in 1966 and was well along in the summer of 1967. But other things were not going so well.

The Cog counted on the pre-season sale of ticket packages that included overnight stays at the Summit House. Dartmouth had sold the Summit House to the state as it had sold the Cog to Col. Teague. He then leased the hotel from the state.

A summit stay had long been part of the allure of a trip up the Cog: Take your family on a steam trip to the top of New England and then stay overnight. Watch the sunset and then awake to see a spectacular summit sunrise. It was on such an overnight that I had first visited the Cog as a small boy.

The ticket packages meant a great deal to the Cog's bottom line. By the spring of 1967, several hundred had been sold. But then politics intervened. State agencies ruled that Teague could not open the Summit House without thousands of dollars in repairs to a water tank, the heating system and sewer systems.

State Parks Director Russell Tobey drew up a funding plan that became a legislative bill. But legislative leaders then insisted that Teague, as lessee, was responsible for the repairs. Tobey said that such major repairs should be paid for by the owner, the State of New Hampshire. Three months of wrangling ensued, and it wasn't until mid-June that the state attorney general ruled that Teague would have to pay.

Tobey said, "No one in his right mind would lease the hotel under these requirements. To make such demands would be to close the whole place down for good. Plain common sense indicates that Col. Teague was never expected to make such major repairs and improvements."

The Teagues were dismayed. They had neither the money nor, at this point, the time to make the repairs the state was ordering. Thousands of dollars in refunds had to be made to disappointed tourists. The Auto Road's owners were also upset, as some of their passengers also booked overnight stays at the Summit House.

Russ Tobey's position in sticking up for Teague was commendable and more than a little surprising given the parks director's views that neither the Cog nor the Auto Road should be allowed to terminate at the summit.

In 1964, Tobey had proposed that the state buy the Auto Road (it wasn't for sale), rip up the Cog tracks at the summit, and relocate the terminus of both to a spot where the Air Force buildings stood. (Tobey was not alone in such sentiments. A 1958 state commission had recommended that the state buy both the road and the Cog and the summit itself.)

Gov. John King put a quick end to Tobey's 1964 plan, telling the Teagues this was a Tobey "trial balloon" that no one else was buying. In 1968, Tobey and others would again propose truncating the Cog and Auto Road, and removing all buildings from the summit. One version of this plan included tourists being conveyed to the top of Mt. Washington through a tunnel.

But this was 1967, and the state's order put a huge dent in Teague's operation. It was one of the reasons that the Teagues were operating without liability insurance, something dangerous for any tourist attraction, let alone one like the Cog Railway.

But the Cog had gone on for so long without a serious accident (dating all the way back to the Peppersass incident for its last fatality) that Art Teague may have been lulled into a false sense of security. Or perhaps his own inner troubles were distracting him.

In any case, the apparent heart attack he suffered that summer is understandable. The Hut had burned, now the state decision was taking crucial dollars from his operation.

Arthur would be in and out of hospitals that summer. He may also have been hospitalized the previous fall in Vermont. The reason was undisclosed. But his daughters believe heart medicine he was taking had contributed to his growing depression.

At one point he was taken to Littleton Hospital for treatment and rest. How much rest he actually got is questionable. Two young men had been hired on as mechanics, even though the shop crew had plenty of those, and the two were left to work on cars. They were let go, to save money. But the two young men were popular, and they were friendly with the Teague girls. Art was a captive audience in the hospital and was prevailed upon to keep the two men employed.

Upon his release, Art was ordered home to his temporary living quarters and a strict regimen of rest.

There had always been ongoing issues with the state and politics and many other challenges, remembers Kevin McKinney, but in his time at the Cog, he didn't notice that any bothered Teague more than others.

"I'm sure they did—but as a great leader, he never showed it."

Art Teague had been that kind of great leader in and since the war. He had carried and supported his men through battle. He had accomplished his objectives. But now, in 1967, the pressures were again great. The life he had built, the family he had raised, all were in jeopardy from forces not as easy to define and target as those from two decades and more before.

Jack Middleton recalls how upset Art was at a board of directors meeting at Marshfield on August 4, 1967. The governor and Executive Council were going to be meeting down the road at the Mt. Washington Hotel that week. It had been Art's tradition, and his great pleasure, to host the VIP group on a trip up the Cog.

He knew it was important to keep the politicians on your side, and he loved showing off the engineering marvel that was the Cog. And with what had happened with the Summit House, along with the earlier state takeover attempts, this trip would be extra important.

But his board reiterated what the doctors had said. Its members were fearful what the strain of the trip, on top of everything else, might do to his heart. The meeting dissolved in argument and was adjourned.

Art was sent home to his cabin. Ellen Teague, accompanied by Middleton and Tony Poltrack, a board member and family friend, went to pay a visit to the Guildhall farm.

It was one of the young men from the south who found Arthur Teague's body.

Steve Christy was from Louisiana. He worked in the shop and on the track crew. He had gone to the Teagues' cabin, expecting to find Ellen Teague. His jeans were so filthy, he said later, that they could stand up by themselves. (He was not alone in that regard. Coggers and their clothes could easily be mistaken for coal miners for much of the summer.)

Christy needed to make a trip to the laundromat in Littleton. He wanted to borrow a vehicle. At the cottage door, he met Lucy Teague, youngest of the Teague daughters, running toward him, saying, over and over, "My father! My father!"

Almost 50 years later, the memory remained vivid for Christy, who was only 18 years old at the time. Lucy had gone to use the bathroom in the little cottage. As she sat down on the toilet, she looked across the room and saw her father.

"There was just a stump of his skull," Christy recalled. For weeks afterward, whenever he closed his eyes, he could not remove that image.

As Christy ran to the shops for help, Claire Dwyer heard Lucy Teague's cries and ran from the girls' dorm to the Teague cabin. She couldn't make out what Lucy, in shock, was saying about her father, but when Lucy led her to the bathroom, she knew.

Claire was secretary in the Cog's office at Marshfield. She said she recognized the colonel only because he was still wearing the same plaid shirt he had worn to the board of directors meeting earlier that day.

Chief mechanic Paul Philbrick, alerted by Christy, came to the cabin and also saw what had befallen his boss.

Word of the suicide ricocheted around the Base Station. The younger people didn't know what to do or where to look, fearful that they, too, would begin to cry. It was for most of them their first experience with sudden, violent death, and they didn't have families to fall back on.

Ellen Teague kept her composure, at least in public. One of her first instructions was to tell Jack Middleton to drive to the nearest pay phone and call my father at the Union Leader. Ellen didn't want the newspaper to report that her husband had taken his life.

My father never told me this story. But he did tell Middleton that Arthur S. Teague was a well-known New Hampshire figure as well as a World War II hero and news of his demise was, well, news.

Arthur Teague was buried in a pretty, tree-crowded cemetery in Lancaster behind the church where his funeral was held. Not all of the Coggers could attend. Trains were still running, although all stopped for a few minutes on the day and hour of his funeral. Tourists were still expecting rides up the mountain.

One special train went up the mountain a few days before the funeral. It was the track train with its flatbed car. Someone had picked out a large rock about the size and shape of a tombstone. The track crew somehow hoisted it up and onto the car and brought it down to Marshfield where it was put on a truck. It became Arthur's headstone, a piece of his mountain now forever near him.

Meanwhile, in the wake of Art's suicide, state officials ran to cover their butts. Now they moved quickly to address the problems that had led to the Summit House shutdown. But that was too late for Art Teague. Within weeks, his tombstone would have a second name added to it.

A few days after finding Art Teague's body, Steve Christy was in his room at the men's boarding house at the end of the day when he heard a commotion. Lucy Teague was keeping her horse with another in a barn on the property, and the two horses were fighting. Little Lucy was trying to separate them.

The effort and noise had attracted Cog crews to the boarding house windows where they were leaning out, laughing at or at least enjoying Lucy's trouble.

Christy, understanding better than anyone what the little girl had just gone through, said to himself, "Well, this is bullshit," and he went to her aid. He knew nothing of horses but he was a big, strong Louisiana teen, and he just grabbed hold of one horse's harness and pulled him away.

Lucy, like her sisters, was an accomplished rider and competitor. Ellen Teague writes in her memoir that it was just two weeks after Art's death that she relented when Anne Teague and her fiancé, Norman Koop, asked to participate in a downstate horse show. They would be taking two horses, including Lucy's. Lucy would go, too, along with her friend, Cindy Lewis, Jitney's daughter.

At some point, driving south on I-93 near Tilton, the horses shifted their weight in the trailer that Norm and Anne were pulling with a car. Over it went. Cindy and Lucy were ejected. Cindy was injured. Lucy was killed.

The Teagues' horrible summer had, unbelievably, gotten worse. Ellen Teague, still composed on the outside, approached Steve Christy and asked him to be a pallbearer at Lucy's funeral. It so happened, she told him, that Lucy had told her mother of how Christy had helped her that day with the unruly horse. She was grateful, Ellen told him.

Unspoken was that it was also Christy who had been the first person

Lucy encountered after finding her father's body. Perhaps that, too, was why she was grateful to the big, soft-spoken Louisiana boy.

My father, shaken by the losses, penned an editorial questioning the "heartless manifestation of the will of an inscrutable providence." He wrote, "Fate, it would appear, selects for its cruelest shafts only the most vulnerable targets."

Of Ellen Teague, he wrote, "famed always for the motherly sweetness and affection which she lavished not only upon her own brood but upon the boys and girls who come every year, from many parts of the country, to work and earn money for their education, on the Cog Railway."

Teague family members, friends, and Coggers gathered again at the same Lancaster church and then trudged up the hill to the same cemetery to lay Lucy's casket beside that of her father.

The few remaining summer weeks went by in a haze for most of us. There was a Cog Party, but it was more a wake. Norm Koop read aloud a poem I had written about Art Teague. It wasn't very good, but it was a sentiment that many shared. Later, Ellen Teague had it inscribed on a brass plaque. For years, it was affixed to a large boulder outside of Marshfield.

In early September, I entered the University of New Hampshire in Durham as a freshman. I didn't know what to expect, and I was not particularly excited or impressed. I did have a friend from the Cog, Gordon Champion, who was also attending. We planned on going back up on a few weekends before the Cog closed for the season.

Then everything changed again.

"One amazing aspect of Art was that he always seemed to be energetic, positive, oriented to solving problems, and taking the time to 'guide and lead' so many young pups who often needed the guiding and the leading, and sometimes a swift kick too—but he never stooped to that nor did he seem upset."—Kevin McKinney, March 2015.

A half-century on, I believe what happened on the mountain on the late afternoon of Sunday, Sept. 17, 1967 was somehow preordained. How long Arthur Teague had been ill, in mind and body, I don't know. But without his full attention to overseeing his complicated business, things had been slipping, even before his heart attack, and it would all come crashing down barely six weeks after his death.

That Sunday in September was a picture-perfect fall day. Everyone said so, even decades later. Hundreds of tourists had taken Cog trains to the summit. So many had extended their stay, rather than returning on the same train, that at 5 p.m. the summit still had more passengers waiting to descend than there was seating available on the last scheduled train down.

Almost 50 years later, there are still discrepancies as to what passengers were told about a "dead-head" or extra train that was being sent up from the base to handle the overload.

In several newspaper accounts, passengers said they had been told that the 56-passenger aluminum Chumley car would be the last one down but a transfer would be made en route for some riders to move to the near-empty train that was on its way up to fetch them.

The state report on the accident that followed notes that the announcement was "that there would be another train coming up to take any other passengers who wished to remain on the mountain."

But it was getting late and people wanted to get down and on their way. The next day was Monday. Work and school called. So people crowded aboard the Chumley car.

The state report notes, "A number of people entered the car which has a seating capacity of 56 persons. It was intended to meet another train at Skyline, where the standees could be transferred in accordance with the usual custom."

I'm not sure what that "usual custom" was in 1967. Years earlier, before Art Teague had installed the Skyline switch, a wooden platform below Skyline was where passengers got off their train and moved to a shuttle for the short ride to the summit.

But on this late afternoon, any standees transferred from the Chumley would end up going back to the summit. At least, that's what the engineer on the dead-head train understood would be happening.

Larry Barrett was making his qualifying run as an engineer on the lightly-loaded train. He told me that his passengers were told no one would be getting off at the summit; they were there strictly to pick up the overload from the Chumley. But they never made it to the top, and it is unclear if any passengers remained at the summit.

As Charley Kenison remembers it, engineer Gordon Chase thought his friend, Frank Thompson, would be bringing up the dead-head and Chase wanted to save Frank some time by getting to Skyline platform first. In fact, it wasn't Frank running the dead-head, and the transfer of passengers never had a chance to take place.

An exact count is unknown, but between 85 and 90 people crowded aboard the Chumley car, filling every seat and with many more standing in the aisle. Within 20 minutes, eight would be dead, including three children, one girl just two years old. Seventy-five to 82 more would be injured.

Gordon Chase had not been Art Teague's best hire. Chase had been in the Army during the war, although where he served I don't know. Why he had lasted so long may have been due in part to the simple fact that he was available in the spring and the fall, when most other engineers were not. Why Chase was still there that September afternoon had, I think, everything to do with Col. Teague no longer being there at all.

Paul Philbrick must have thought so. It would come out years later that he held himself partly responsible for the accident. Devoted to Teague, Paul fought with Ellen Teague and departed the Cog soon after Art's death.

Paul had stayed with the J.D. True family in Skagway, Alaska. In a letter to Jitney Lewis after Paul's death, True wrote: "He had convinced the boss to give that engineer involved (in the crash) another chance after being fired so one just figured this was why the different moods."

The "boss" was most likely Ellen Teague. In a series of letters to Jitney from Alaska, Paul was sharply critical of Mrs. Teague. He predicted she would promote one of her family to manage the Cog, that she would have to borrow money, and that she would eventually have to sell out to the State of New Hampshire, and that coal-fired engines would be replaced by diesel. His one prediction to come to pass has been the near-elimination of steam trains.

Jitney Lewis would hear the news of the accident on television. He had left for the season after the car accident that had injured his daughter and killed Lucy Teague.

Jitney told his son, Tim, that he had never qualified Chase to be an engineer. Yet there Chase was when I arrived in 1965 and there he was two years later, running an overloaded train with an inexperienced crew on a lovely fall day.

Chase usually ran the Number 1 engine, the Mt. Washington. But things change in the fall. Engines and cars, like crews, are swapped out of service for repair and winter storage.

On this day, Chase was in charge of the 3 engine, the Base Station. I had been the 3's brakeman a year earlier, with Lincoln school teacher Griff Harris running. This day, Harris was running another engine. Margie Teague's fiancé, Tom Baker, was braking for Harris.

Chase was no Griff Harris. He had a rookie brakeman (Nat Carter) on the overcrowded car, and he had his fireman, Charley Kenison, sitting in the engineer's seat.

Also in the cab were Rusty Aertsen, who was a brakeman but had fired that trip, and Nat Carter's brother, Peter, another Cogger who was on a busman's holiday with his girlfriend, who was aboard the Chumley. It was Peter's 20th birthday.

Engines always slowed when going through a switch. That was especially the case for down coming trains at the steep Skyline switch.

But this time, the switch at Skyline had been improperly thrown. A key short piece of rail that went over the main line cog rack to form the siding rail was in that position. You can see it in newspaper and police photographs taken the next day. It had been mangled from the force of first the engine and then the weight of the overloaded car going over it.

When Chase's engine hit the rail, the force lifted it up into the air and when it fell back, it tottered for a second and then, slammed by the overloaded car, it toppled off the track to the right on the down-mountain side.

This was extraordinary. The engine and its tender weigh about 18 tons. No one had ever seen anything like this since the Peppersass crackup of 40 years earlier. Eerily, the times were almost the same. The Peppersass had begun its fatal descent at 5 p.m.

Kenison remembers: "Peter (Carter) was told to get in the cab. Chase deemed that Nat had had enough training. I was told that I was running and he was going to make me an engineer (like him!).

"I had only run from the standpipe to the bunker with Dave Gordon before that. (While we did Chase's job and he sat at the ticket office) The last thing that I remember is Chase screaming in my face because I was slowing down coming into the switch. Obviously no one was looking at the switch. When we hit, Chase and I wound up the brake and stopped. I think Peter and Rusty jumped at some point. Then the coach slammed into us and over we went."

Fifty years on, Aertsen remembers.

"On the way down, I was sitting in the fireman's seat looking back at Nat—it was an aluminum car. This was my first trip with Chase and I remember he was going very fast.

"I remember the engine going up, like when you drive too fast over a speed bump. The next think I knew the engine was on its side and the cab was split open. I couldn't see the car. I hit a rock on the way out so I ended up in Littleton Hospital."

In Philadelphia, Aertsen's father was told that his son was dead.

"The local papers had me listed as dead and my dad drove up thinking that was the case until he saw me at the hospital," Aertsen said.

Aertsen thought the train would be moving onto the Skyline switch for the upcoming train.

"I was told that Nat had jumped back on the car and set the brakes so the car didn't go into Burt's Ravine. There is no question in my mind that the stop-before-you-proceed rule (a rule ordered by the state after the accident) would have prevented this, even with Chase at the helm."

Peter Carter's memory is that their train wouldn't be going on the Skyline siding, that it was the last train going down, and that his brother, since deceased, did not get off to throw the switch.

A car by itself can weigh five tons. With its overload, this one weighed much more. The weight was apparently no problem on the way down from the summit to Skyline. Nat Carter told state investigators he used just one of the two brakes and all was well. But the extra weight may have added to the speed of the engine as Carter released the car brake entering the switch.

Nat Carter didn't think so. He told the state that his speed down the mountain was normal and that the engine slowed, as usual, entering the switch. Moments later, however, he saw the engine "pop up and down" and derail. He applied the left brake while a tourist moved to turn the right brake.

Carter said the car nearly stopped but then it, too, hit the mis-thrown rail and picked up speed. With the car partially derailed, the brakes were now useless.

Why a car so overloaded was allowed to leave the summit, even for a short distance, is hard to understand, unless you knew Gordon Chase. Heedless of safety concerns, he let an inexperienced brakeman deal with the crowd of tourists, all of whom surged onto his train.

I have come to believe that it was all of a piece with Arthur Teague's illness and death and the aftermath that left the Cog's operations in disarray. Had the colonel lived, he would have been overseeing operations, especially in the fall with his main men, such as Jitney Lewis and Bob Kent, gone for the season. And a healthy Arthur Teague, who had made battlefield decisions and knew his men, might have already let Chase go.

The state report notes that Chase couldn't understand why he didn't notice the wrongly-flipped rail. Kenison and Aertsen also didn't notice it. But now there was a steam engine on its side and a half-on, half-off overloaded passenger car careening down the mountain, just as Larry Barrett's dead-head train pitched up over a crest at what is known as Long Trestle. People on each train could see the other.

The derailed Chumley car kept sliding down mountain.

"It was panic. People were screaming," Army Pfc. Harry Roemish, 24, of Hinckley, Ohio, said at the time. He and his wife, Pam, vacationing in New Hampshire, were aboard the Chumley train that Sunday afternoon.

"We hit the siding and it threw the engine off. It rolled off the track and we kept going down the hill. People were trying to kick out the windows—everyone could see what was happening."

He added, "We were really flying. The guys who jumped out the windows got hurt real bad. Then the car went off the track and slipped to the right . . . I landed on my back and people were on top of me. I either fell through the window or the floor."

The weight of the people at the down-mountain end of the car finally forced it off the track entirely. The aluminum car, one of two that Arthur Teague had designed and built after the war to accommodate his growing business, lay split open against the jagged rocks on the mountainside.

While several newspaper accounts at the time, including my own, make mention of the two trains, the near-miss angle went unnoticed in the reporting and in the state report. The dead-head train had 19 passengers aboard. Some passengers said the two trains were fewer than 300 yards apart when the Chumley finally flipped over.

Barrett was qualifying as an engineer under Pliney Granger III. He remembers seeing something out of the corner of his eye. As he began stopping the engine, his brakeman jumped off the car (quite a feat on Long Trestle) and yelled for him to stop.

Barrett stopped and used a track phone to call to the base, saying the Number 3 engine was on its side but that he couldn't see the Chumley car. From his angle, on the right side of his cab looking up, his view would be blocked.

Ralph Shackett, a passenger on the upbound train, said his attention had been caught by a sudden "big puff of smoke right in front of us."

"I saw the car go shooting off into space. When it landed, it was lucky it didn't go farther because it would have rolled three miles if it got going."

Shackett followed the brakeman from the upbound train as he ran up the track. "I first saw people climbing out from broken windows.

"People were scattered all over the rocky ground, bleeding and in shock. Some were wandering around. I saw a man and woman whose child lay dead beside them, helping a bleeding victim."

A dazed survivor stumbled down toward Barrett's train, asking for jackets and sweaters to warm the injured. "Receiving no response at first," the

Union Leader reported, "he told them, 'My little boy (age 3) is lying dead back there, won't you help me?'"

Other passengers had crawled from the wreckage and were stumbling about. Moans could be heard, muffled by the wind on the mountain, now seeing its last daylight slipping away. A passenger later looked at his watch, which had smashed. The time read 5:26 p.m.

Pliney Granger stood watch over the dead-head train while Barrett made his way to the crash site. The experience changed his life. He would become an Emergency Medical Technician. But his first triage experience was that afternoon helping a doctor.

Sports car buff Dr. Francis Appleton of Gorham had driven his Jaguar up the Auto Road that Sunday afternoon—in just 12 minutes. Preparing to go back down (he already had his seat belt on), he was told of the crash. He grabbed his black bag and ran down the grease-slicked tracks to help. He would stay until the last of the injured had been removed.

Barrett heard and saw the worst. The Chumley was leaning on its side, with some people beneath it. He remembers picking up a stringer (one of the 20-foot timbers used to support the track bed) and jamming it to keep the car from falling farther. Sheer adrenaline must have taken over.

Ellen Teague would write of directing employees at the base to bring up the flatbed track car, the same one that had been used to carry down Art Teague's gravestone. Her nurse training kicking in, she told them to round up all the pillows and bedding they could find and head up to the crash scene. She then drove down to Fabyans to the nearest phone booth and began alerting hospitals, doctors, police and the state Public Utilities Commission.

The crash had cut the base-to-summit phone line. Barrett, using two track phones above and below the cut, relayed information between base and summit. He remembers State Trooper John Tholl (later a state legislator) driving all the way from Troop F in Twin Mountain, around and up the Auto Road, and then running down to the crash site.

He, Barrett and others guided the wounded and daze passengers to the dead-head's car. A woman, cradling her infant, refused to board. She told Barrett she would rather walk to the summit.

Barrett spoke with her and she finally agreed to board, on one condition. She wanted Barrett to be the brakeman on the trip down. He agreed. Pliney Granger ran the engine.

In Littleton, Dr. Harry McDade readied an emergency team that extended across several hospitals in the North Country. McDade, already something of a legend for his work in attending to hikers and others injured in the White Mountains, would add immeasurably to his story that night. (He and Dr. Appleton, who had followed the injured off, and others would be commended by the state.)

Cogger Tom Norcott was among those who rode up on the flatbed. He said he tried to avoid going.

"I tried to talk my way out of it because of what I had heard on the (track phone) radios about the carnage, but was told there was no option to avoid the rescue. I remember arriving at the scene and seeing Gordie Chase who was in a state of shock as was Charley Kenison.

"Gordie's hands were badly burned with long shreds of skin hanging from his hands and fingers. Charlie was burned and in shock too. It was chaotic . . . Folks crying and screaming and running around bleeding and in shock."

Survivors, some badly injured, were loaded onto the flatbed and the dead-head train for the descent. Norcott got into the cab of the dead-head's engine and sat in the coal tender. It was now dark. In the distance, he could see the lights of ambulances and other cars lined up along the base road.

Dan Noel, a member of the North Conway Rescue Squad, told the Associated Press in 2007 that, "he remembered that many people had substantial injuries like broken arms and legs."

"'The first train down with the injured—they were stacked like cordwood," he recalled. "The thing that stuck in my mind was a man came up to me, and he said, 'Gosh, can you make sure that my daughter gets off the mountain?'" Noel recalled. "And I said, 'Yes, all the injured people, they're taking them in the order of the severity of injury,' and he said, 'No, you don't understand. My daughter's dead. I just don't want her lying up there overnight.'"

For Norcott, the scene at the base was nearly as chaotic as what he had seen on the mountain.

"More crying, fear and many folks wondering if their loved ones were alive."

He met an older couple looking lost and confused. They had waited at the base while their son and grandchildren took the ride to the top. Norcott offered to take them to the hospital in Littleton. Their son was a doctor. He had broken his back in the crash, and his daughter had been pinned under the overturned car. She was not breathing.

The father crawled on his stomach and dug out the cinders from around her and gave her CPR. She survived, as did her brother, who was also injured.

Weeks earlier, after Arthur's suicide, Jack Middleton had convinced Ellen Teague that she must get liability insurance for the railway. She gave him the okay, reluctantly, and Middleton was able to purchase a $1.1 million policy. It was enough, in 1967, to settle all the death and injury claims. They were lucky.

Ellen Teague writes in her book that a veteran Cog engineer testified before the Public Utilities Commission that on the first run up the mountain some mornings, he would sometimes find a switch tampered with, presumably by hikers. The Appalachian Mountain Club trail crossed the tracks not far from Skyline.

Such switch tampering is certainly possible. There is no security mechanism to prevent it. But in my own years working there, and in all the time I have been in touch with other crew members, I never saw or heard of such an occurrence.

There have been a few occasions when a brakeman, racing to keep up with his train or showing off, has accidentally missed flipping a rail. But the last train through Skyline switch before the accident had two people throwing the switch: Tom Baker and Nick Chaykowski. Nick was a local Cogger from Berlin. It was Nick who had accompanied Tom on the long walk down the tracks from the summit the day that Arthur Teague had died.

The two told state investigators that Tom was showing Nick how to brake and that they had been particularly careful in throwing Skyline.

Human error? For sure. But whether from the previous train crew or from a hiker, the fact is that Gordon Chase should have checked the switch as he was descending. I doubt he ever did so, and at the speed he was going, he might have missed it even had he been looking. Faster, he had told Kenison.

Aertsen and Kenison, along with Chase, said they looked at the switch and it appeared in the correct position.

In his book, "Railway to the Moon," author Glen Kidder writes that "at a little distance, it is very difficult to make out much in the way of detail between the rails since the center cog rail usually is covered with grease and appears dark and therefore not very distinct.

"This situation is likely to be more obvious in the latter part of the day when the light is not so good. Thus the misplaced section of the cog rail might not have been readily apparent to the engine crew from their positions in the cab."

The state PUC report concludes that the misplaced rail was the cause and that, "The failure of those on the engine to notice this, in view of the fact that they looked at it as the train approached, is very difficult to explain. Had it been noticed and the train stopped before striking it, the accident would not have occurred."

Kidder and others also advance the idea that the overcrowded car actually saved lives and injuries because the passengers were so packed in as to cushion each other when the Chumley flipped off the track.

Post-accident, the PUC would mandate that all trains come to a full stop at the mountainside switches and that the brakeman check the switch before waving the train through.

Arthur Teague had designed much longer switch-outs, where trains could meet and pass each other in parallel, making the procedure much less subject to accident. He did not live to see them, but such a switch-out is now in place at Waumbek, with another planned for Skyline. Solar-powered, it requires little human action.

I left UNH and headed for the Cog after hearing of the crash. I wanted to help. I also wanted a reason to quit college. There wasn't much to be done at the Cog. Post-Labor Day, only weekend trains ran and with the crash, even those had been temporarily halted. But this was the Cog. One fatal accident in 60 years? Why should that stop the trains?

Ellen Teague writes that it was very uncertain if the trains would run again that year. But the PUC allowed it, based on the preliminary finding of "human error" rather than mechanical problem.

The decision was based, too, on the pressure the state was getting from North Country tourist attractions. The Cog was the big draw. With the foliage season peaking, other attractions feared losing out if tourists heard that the Cog wasn't running.

I came home, depressed by all that had happened that summer and still looking to convince myself that college wasn't right for me. I didn't need much convincing. My father disagreed but did see how upset I was. He invited me to a meeting of the newspaper's reader advisory board where Publisher William Loeb asked me to explain the Cog and what I knew of the accident.

People seemed genuinely interested in what I had to say and, surprise to me, accepted as gospel what I was telling them about my summer job, which had now turned deadly.

Reluctantly, I went back to UNH. I also went back to work part-time in the paper's sports department. But the most memorable year of 1967 still had one more Cog-related surprise for me.

Gordon Champion and I had arranged to spend Thanksgiving in Philadelphia, home base for the Teagues and many Coggers, including Claire Dwyer, whom I was dating.

I stayed at Claire's house and had Thanksgiving dinner with her family. The next morning, I was positive that Mrs. Dwyer had found me not good enough for her daughter and had poisoned me with her turkey.

After dinner, several of us went to play touch football in back of Norm Koop's home but after a couple of plays, he saw I was in pain. He took me inside where his father, future U.S. Surgeon General Dr. C. Everett

Koop, had me lie down on his living room rug. The quick diagnosis: acute appendicitis.

"You are one of the New Hampshire boys?" Dr. Koop asked.

I nodded.

"When are you returning home?"

I told him, "Tomorrow."

"No, no," he said, in a matter of fact tone as he glanced at his watch. "Your appendix is going to rupture in about four hours. Norm, get this young man to the hospital."

Chestnut Hill Hospital on Germantown Ave. is a small facility. I am told the surgeon questioned my anesthesia since, as he stood over me, scalpel in hand, I looked up and said, "Aren't you supposed to hold that over a match?"

I convalesced in the maternity ward. As I say, it was a small hospital.

In December, the year ended in a better note. Tom Baker married Margie Teague in Concord, N.H.

Chapter 7

LAST YEAR

Author Joe McQuaid would run the "Deuce" with fireman
Gordon Champion and brakeman Ray Clark in 1968.

THE NEXT YEAR, 1968, would be my last at the Cog. It began with what seemed a resumption of the terrible year before. David Koop was Norm's younger brother and a student at Dartmouth College. He had worked with us at the Cog and was a favorite of all who knew him, with a funny smile and a genuine, kind manner.

He and a friend had spent a Sunday in April, 1968, rock climbing on Cannon Mountain.

Cannon, famed for its ski slopes (it was where Bode Miller would train) and Old Man of the Mountain profile, also had challenging sheer-granite cliffs that drew experienced hikers. Dave Koop was one of them. But on this day, climbing above his partner, he hollered back that there was a loose rock ahead of him, one the size of a car.

Moments later, that rock dropped, slamming into Koop. He tumbled past his partner who luckily was able to stop his own motion and Koop's. He climbed down and got Koop to a 14-inch wide ledge. Koop was bleeding badly from a shattered leg. He lost consciousness and died on the mountain.

Paul Philbrick had always been the first man into the base each spring. Knowing he wasn't returning after the terrible summer of '67, he had left detailed hand-written instructions on how to get the power on and the shop machines running. It was spring break at UNH and I jumped at the chance when Tom Baker invited me to help him.

Tom and I stayed at the boarding house, taking our meals with Crawford Hassen, who loved tweaking Tom about his mother-in-law, Ellen Crawford Teague, and trying to engage me in philosophical discussions.

It was one of the earliest springs the White Mountains had seen in years, setting high temperature records in Concord. It made the work even more pleasant for me, though just the chance of being back at the Cog and away from school did that.

We hiked up Franklin Brook, following Paul's directions, to find keys and gear that channeled a powerful current to activate the Pelton water wheel that Arthur Teague had installed in the shops years before. It amazed me then and now at how men like Sylvester Marsh and Arthur Teague had adapted modern engineering to the wilds of the White Mountains.

I don't remember having any doubts, when the school year ended, of heading back to the Cog for another summer.

Jitney Lewis was no longer there, but my memory is that he had told Joe Long and me that the colonel had plans for us to qualify as engineers. It didn't surprise me about Joe Long. The Philadelphia boy who couldn't pronounce "cowlick" (with his accent, he actually thought it was a "kal-lick") had adapted easily to braking and firing and seemed to understand mechanics, certainly better than I. I just knew if you moved this big wheel, the engine would go forward.

Joe got his chance first and nearly blew it, thanks to a finicky water injector that just wouldn't stay open for him as he left the Base Station on his first trip up.

You need to keep water pumping into the boiler to make steam. I knew that much. The water is sucked in from the tender through rubber hoses. It is done through a process so bizarre that the U.S. patent office engineer assigned to review it didn't believe it until he saw it with his own eyes.

To this day, I couldn't explain how it works, but it involves creating a vacuum that sucks up the water. You know it's working by touching your bare hand to the water pipe. If it's cold, water is feeding into the boiler. If it's not, you are getting steam, which means your injector hasn't worked or it has worked but then "broken" at some point. Oh, and you burn your hand on the pipe.

Joe Long may actually have understood the injector concept. But I had a knack for getting an injector to go on and stay on. And I knew how to check one regularly. I could also spit well. If the spit evaporated on the pipe, you were in trouble.

I watched Joe proudly blow the engine whistle and chug up the first trestle over the Ammonoosuc River. And then stop. And sit there, for what seemed like forever as he tried desperately to get the injector to work.

He was probably under the watchful eye of Frank Thompson, who, unlike Gordon Chase, took care of his engine, and took care of his crew. Either Frank or Joe finally got the injector to take, and off they went.

I don't remember who was riding with me when I qualified, but I imagine it was Bud Nye. Bud was a steady hand in any situation. In my last year there, Ellen Teague let Bud move from the boarding house to a cabin usually reserved for engineers and their families. Bud had been pre-med in college and was studying for entrance to medical school. He would succeed.

Among the Cog connections that came from friends of friends were Steve Christy and Lee Fisher. Christy had told his fellow Louisianan about the Cog. Lee was intrigued and thought it might be a better way of earning money then on a shrimp boat for the summer.

Fisher came north, remembering the cold, foggy weather that greeted the two in Littleton in June and the hard work that would follow on the track crew that summer.

What happened to Fisher on that crew and the life story he had thereafter is remarkable as well. Somehow, Fisher was in the wrong place on a track crew when a stringer, one of the main supporting timbers on which the rails ran, slipped and struck him full on the neck.

He was unable to feel his limbs. Bud Nye, now in med school, was there. He told the crew to get Fisher flat on a board. He then called down to the base, telling them to have an ambulance there when the train got down.

Fisher was taken to Littleton Hospital where personnel realized this was not a case for them. On the "slowest ride of my life," Fisher was sent by ambulance to Mary Hitchcock Hospital in Hanover. He had no feeling for 10 days. A doctor used an experimental injection to prevent movement of his spine. Dr. Koop stopped by to assure the boy he was in good hands.

Ellen Teague was with Koop. She told Fisher that the Cog would do whatever he wished, whether have him flown home to Louisiana or fly his parents up. Fisher said he didn't need either. He said he was going to walk and go back to work at the Cog.

And miraculously he did. Two years later, with a low draft number, he signed up for the U.S. Air Force., spending five years flying medevac choppers before transferring to F4 fighters for a 20-year plus career. If Col. Teague were looking down, he must have been pleased to see a fellow Cogger succeeding in the military that had meant so much to him.

Lee Fisher's Cog buddy, Steve Christy, would also learn to fly planes. But he did it as an avocation, staying on in New Hampshire and becoming president of a bank in the state's upper valley.

Dr. Glenn "Bud" Nye would become a cardiologist and heart surgeon. He worked with Physicians for Peace, organizing groups that worked in Egypt, Jordan, Yemen and the Palestine territories. He helped doctors in Syria and Palestine performed their first angioplasties. Bud had brought his chum, Tim Bemis, to the Cog his second year. The next year, they brought another teen from their Philly neighborhood, Norm Koop, to the White Mountains with them.

After leaving for Alaska, Paul Philbrick didn't appear to care too much about anything. After his death, J.D. True explained to Jitney Lewis:

"During the winter of 1970 during a blizzard he left the house in his Jeep—to where we didn't know. Many hours later and dark, we drove out the road a ways but couldn't tell anything for several inches of new snow," they wrote. "Sometime later, we got a phone call from the pipeline pump station and 1-and-a-half miles from here. Paul had parked out on the river-bed about 3 miles out and hiked into the storm. When he returned the Jeep wouldn't start on account of frozen gas line. He attempted to correct the situation and got gas on his hands. He must have lost his sense of reason for one of his mitts was still there. He hiked the 1-and-a-half or two miles to the pump station and froze his hands really bad. I don't remember how long he was in the Juneau hospital but all his fingers had to be amputated.

"He returned from the hospital and back to his job. I know he must have a real problem trying to do machine work with no fingers and as I remember he was really depressed."

In August 1971, Paul "left one morning in his Jeep (I don't remember whether he told us or not whether he didn't plan to work)—About 2 p.m.,

I think, Anna noticed a note by the phone. All it said was 'I will be where I was hurt.' Anna and a friend went out to the riverbed where he'd frozen his hands" and there they found Paul had shot himself in the head with a rifle, as Arthur Teague had done just four years and thirteen days before.

"It was quite a blow to us for we really thought well of him," wrote Mr. True. "Anna and I made a trip back to see Paul's family that fall. His parents in Mexico, Maine—a sister in Rutland, Vermont and brother in Natick, Mass. Paul's family are really nice people and we are glad we made that trip. Hope this gives a little as to what happened—It was sad indeed."

Paul Philbrick was just 35.

Charlie Teague was a good-looking boy with dirty blond hair, a soft voice, and a pleasant smile. He looked like his dad, and he was treated as the natural male heir, destined to learn the ropes and eventually run the railway. He was coddled by his mother and sisters, humored or ignored by the train crews, and left to do as he pleased for much of his childhood summer days.

After Arthur's death, and even after it had become clear to most everyone that Charlie was mentally ill, Ellen was telling friends that "Charles" was the person to help her run the place. For a time, he tried, learning how to run the engines and helping with general operations. But by the time she sold the railroad in 1983 Charlie went with her.

Years later, I got word from one of her daughters that Ellen was in failing health and would like to see me. I drove up one late summer day to visit them at their modest home near a small lake in Whitefield. Ellen had suffered a series of heart attacks and had lost eldest daughter, Jane, to complications from diabetes. This day, she was all about the memories, especially of her "boys." Charlie proudly showed me his father's medals from the war. But he said little.

Ellen Teague died in 1999, her funeral held in the same Lancaster church from where she had buried her husband and two daughters. She lies with them in the peaceful cemetery in Lancaster. Charlie Teague lives in a group home in Vermont. His surviving three sisters visit him from time to time.

My own years at the Cog ended in 1968. The next spring, a new minor league baseball team moved to Manchester and I was assigned to cover its summer season. I guess I knew that this was another step in what would be my newspaper career. But it was still not an easy decision. I called Mrs. Teague, who was at her Philadelphia home, to break the news.

She was gracious, as always. I understand now that while a big deal for me, it was not exactly earth-shattering news to the woman who had spent much of her life looking after hundreds of boys that she and Arthur Teague had brought to the mountains and, in many ways, to manhood.

The Mt. Washington Cog Railway is the world's first mountain-climbing cog (rack-and-pinion) railway. It is the second steepest, with its sharpest grade, on Jacob's Ladder, is 37.41 percent. The average grade is 25 percent.

It has been recognized by engineering societies as one of man's finest achievements. The American Societies of Mechanical and Civil Engineering have designated the Cog a national historic landmark. Those involved with the preservation of steam power have been especially proud of it. An effort by state and EPA bureaucrats to stop the coal-burning trains in the 1970s was met by near-unanimous contempt by the New Hampshire legislature, which passed specific language exempting the Cog from pollution limits.

Arthur S. Teague, having run the Cog for Dartmouth College in the 1950s after Henry Teague's death, purchased the railway in 1962. Tim Lewis notes, that "eighteen months before the sale, Col. Teague told Cincinnati Enquirer reporter Dave Roberts that he would never convert the Cog to diesel or electric power.

"'Part of the attractiveness of our mountain railroad are the white steam puffs from the stacks of our oddly shaped locomotives,' said Teague. 'And I mean to keep it that way.'"

Teague had told New Yorker reporter at large, Phil Hamburger, the same thing in 1959.

"I'll never give up steam," said Teague. "Out west, on Pike's Peak, there's a cog railway that has diesels, but never on Mount Washington. No, sir! It wouldn't be the same without steam, even if there is some soot and noise. That's part of the charm and the thrill. We use a ton of coal for each trip to the top. It costs me seven dollars a ton at the mine, in West Virginia, and nine dollars a ton to ship it here."

Today, one wonders if the protections offered the Cog through the last 150 years will continue. The Cog has few remaining steam engines. One of them sits atop a knoll in Twin Mountain, serving as a promotional sign for the railway. A few others are maintained for the single coal-fired steam train that still runs daily up the mountain. Other trips are by means of diesel engines, introduced in 2008. One of the old wooden passenger cars was airlifted to a spot on a ski trail at nearby Bretton Woods where it serves as a warming hut.

In late 2016, longtime co-owners Joel and Cathy Bedor and Wayne Presby announced a plan for a luxury hotel to be built at or perhaps over the Skyline switch. In the spring of 2017, the Bedors sold their Cog interest to Presby.

Chapter 8

ARTHUR S. TEAGUE

Commanding Officer 22nd Infantry
4th Infantry Division

LT. COLONEL ARTHUR S. TEAGUE'S 3rd Battalion, 22nd Infantry Regiment, was initially attached to the Eighth Infantry Regiment. Teague's first-person account of his first days and nights after hitting the beach at Normandy is reproduced here.

June 6–8, 1944

From landing craft we came ashore on LCM's (Landing Craft Mechanized)—three of them—operated by Navy enlisted men. One of the enlisted men on our LCM remarked that this was the third landing in which he had participated and that he didn't mind the initial landing so much as he did the ones afterwards because he would have to keep bringing in supplies.

Just as we were coming in to the shore I saw a shell that was fired from up the beach, and I knew some of us were going to be hit. I could see the spurts of water coming up. I saw one small landing craft hit, and thinking the same might happen to us, I told the Navy man to ram the beach as hard as possible. He said he would, and after holding it wide open for about two hundred yards, we hit the beach and stepped off on dry soil. A couple of boats behind us—about seventy-five yards back in the water—were hit, and then I saw a number of casualties. Many were killed and quite a few wounded.

I started up by the sea wall on the sand dunes and stopped for a moment, and it was then that I heard someone call me. It was General Roosevelt. He called me over and told me we had landed 'way to the left of where we were supposed to have landed, and that he wanted us to get this part of the beach cleared as soon as possible. He wanted action from my men immediately after landing, and asked me to get them down the beach as soon as I could. This was about 0930.

At this time we were getting quite a bit of artillery fire from the inland side of the beach. It was not very heavy, but spasmodic. I went on over and called a couple of officers on the staff and got behind the sea wall and suggested that we figure out what we had to do. We talked it over and thought about what could happen and decided the best thing to do was to find Captain Samuels, the Company Commander, and see what troops were already on the beach so that we could take stock of them.

A couple of tanks were on the beach and I yelled to one and crawled up on it. I asked the enlisted men about firing on the beach on the troops we could see. He stated that he had strict orders to just sit there and protect the troops coming ashore, and that was all. I told him for God's sake to start fire so we could reduce the troops waiting for us. He said he had orders to defend until the troops went through.

We started up the beach and I hollered back to everybody and got them dissembled because I saw two men who were lost on mines. I stayed on the sand dunes to see if I could identify my location on the map. Standing with my back to the water, looking inland, a little bit to my right front was the little round windmill or silo standing up which I had observed on aerial photographs and panoramic views of the beach before, which gave me the immediate location of where we were. I tried to get higher on the sand dunes, but someone yelled at me that snipers were firing and for me to come down.

I started on up the beach wall and ran into more troops and they said Lt. Tolles had been shot. On my way there, I passed along a number of baby tanks which had electrical wiring and were loaded with TNT. Some troops wanted to fire into one and I told them to stop that action, and I posted guards on it. I went on around this little firing trench marked by barbed wire and sandy beach grass. Near this firing trench I went behind a sand dune into an open place and found Lt. Tolles lying on his side near another wounded man. I asked him what happened and he said he saw a white flag and he tried to get them to surrender and someone had fired on him. I immediately sent someone back to notify a doctor to move him out of the place. I went further up and ran into member s of his platoon who had stopped and were having quite a little rifle fire back and forth. I saw what was happening as they moved along. My German interpreter was with me. We ran and hollered to them and he yelled to the enemy in German. I ran on top of the sand dune. There I picked up an M-I rifle and called to our men to get going. We went forward and suddenly encountered direct fire. I saw two Germans wounded. About seventeen of them raised up from different places around and started running across the beach. Pvt. Meis yelled at them in German. I questioned them and asked them where their mines were and about the number of Germans. They said they didn't know—that they had come only the night before. I told them they did know and that they would go with us.

I then started a skirmish line up the beach. They went about fifty yards. up the beach and yelled. "Mine!" They started showing paths we could take to get out of there. I had seen Lt. Burton and Sgt. McGee wounded by mines along the beach. We moved on down the beach and picked up about 40 more Germans. Where they came from I do not know; evidently troops ran them out. They came with their hands up and ran down the beach. We got on up a little farther and ran into a steel gate which I thought was a T-7 entrance but now believe it to have been an entrance to U-5 causeway. I got hold of Lt. Ramano, Engineer Platoon Leader, and told him to open up the gate and while he was doing it, to have his engineers go up ahead and to lift out any mines.

I had gone up the beach a little farther and heard that my tanks were ashore so I sent someone down there to get ahold of the tanks and to tell them to come on down the beach. This A Platoon, under command of a lieutenant from Alabama—I've forgotten his name—came up the beach about this time and we ran across from the little fortification on the beach wall. The Germans were firing down the beach a little and I could see these shots were hitting in the water. Some skimmed the tops of our heads and some hit small boats. One of our tanks came up and got fired on and hit by small caliber guns. It was then that we noticed a small steel turret mounted on top of a pillbox, and was moving along behind the beach wall. Our tank was about twenty-five yards away, but it immediately elevated its guns and opened fire, knocking the turret completely off the little fortification. Here we got quite a few more prisoners.

In the meantime, our men were having a pretty good fight inland near an old French fort where they had taken about a hundred prisoners. As we pushed on up the beach our tanks were firing along the whole time. We found another steel gate of the Belgian type near the beach. It had been used quite a bit by vehicles before we landed. I positively identified it myself as being near T-7. I told Lt. Manor to get that out of the way. I had a tank. I pointed the gates out and he opened that entrance. I waited until he finished the job.

I continued on up the beach right in behind several units of our company and ran into Captain Samuels. Captain Samuels talked about one of the little tanks which had pushed around the entrance to T-7 and had stopped and been fired upon about three times by guns. The shots ricocheted off the tank and the Lieutenant fired the first shot, which went through the pillbox, which was the fortification we were supposed to have landed in front of. About twenty-five Germans ran across the beach with their hands up. The companies pushed on to the fortification, and there I was with Captain Samuels, Captain Walker, and almost all the battalion staff. Major Goforth joined us and had I Company to hold up this point and L Company to attack normal buildings and the entrance to Causeway S- 9. The attack was supplementary. At the time we were getting mortar fire, so we three officers, plus Pvt. Buchavellis, decided we would dig into the sand dunes on Tare Green Beach. We dug about two feet in the sand and finally I remarked that that wasn't going to do any good because we weren't getting any of the other fortifications.

We kept noticing the gunfire that was coming down the beach so I took the platoon leader, and he and I crawled down the beach to see if we could observe where they were firing from. While we were lying there the Germans saw us and fired two shots. One went over our heads and hit the water. The next one ricocheted off the tank which was close to us. We called for another tank. Firing continued from the S-9 fortification causing quite a few casualties. Our tank fired a few rounds at it and finally destroyed it.

The mortar fire had let up a little by this time, which had been coming down from up the beach. I had just learned that one of our men with
a flamethrower ran about twenty-five Germans out of a pillbox. He had
taken two American paratroopers from that same pillbox.

I started out from this fortification straight across the minefield. I saw a
house on fire. Behind me was Captain Walker and Captain Williams and
quite a string of men. As we walked across this area, which had been dry
at the time the mines had been placed in the ground, we could see several
places which we knew mines were in, because we could see where rocks had
been prized up. I took out some white engineer's tape which we all carried,
and we marked them as we went. I told them to step in the same tracks
that I had made. As we walked I heard one explode behind me. Captain
Williams hit it and he got it through the cheek of the buttocks.

We went on across the mine field and found L Company, Here we met
Captain Blazzard, who had machine guns set up and had been firing. I
ordered them to assault the house and the S-9 nest simultaneously. This
was a matter of about thirty minutes. I yelled for Captain Ernest to get
him to hold L Company because I wanted to send K Company into attack.

All this time there was a gun still firing up the beach. It later developed
that we could see where two or three shots hit the embrasures, but the
Germans had destroyed it themselves.

About this time I told Captain Ernest we could make an attack on the
water's edge. We went out on the S-9 fortification about two hundred
yards. The roads seemed to be in excellent shape, showing they had been
used. We found a French civilian in one of the houses, so we asked him
where the mines were. He pointed out that the road from S-9 up the beach
was mined. In fact, he showed me about eight or ten mines. You could see
where the mines had been put under the rocks. He said that the road hadn't
been used for about four months. He said the other road was being used,
and, to the best of his knowledge, was not mined.

We pushed around for a short time and K Company jumped off and
made a flank attack. I went with a battalion staff behind K Company. I
started wading in water up to my waist, and in some places, up to my
armpits. A long column of men was wading through the water. A sniper

got a man just ahead of me. He lay for most of the whole night because he couldn't be evacuated.

I followed K Company on up and encountered Lt. Pruzinski. He talked to Captain Ernest and told him that there was supposed to be a flame thrower behind the house, so I sent the Lieutenant out.

Then we went on up the beach and hit the causeway. We were getting quite a bit of fire and also quite a bit of mortar. Finally K Company was able to take the approach to the causeway. Lt. Pruzinski had two tanks and he captured that point.

K Company cleared out the causeway and a few buildings at the end of it, and as it got late at night, I told Captain Ernest that we couldn't make much more distance, and we made preparations for the night.

There was a house there which we were afraid might be a booby trap. The men began digging into the place, but it was flooded with water. We were getting machine gun fire from the fortification ahead of us, so I told Captain Ernest that since we couldn't dig in, we would sleep along the road and I would stay with the group. We lay down sometime around 12:30 at night, although it was hardly dark. We stayed there for the night. Captain Ernest, Captain Walker and Major Goforth were with me. I told Ernest to tell the men we could sleep there tonight and that we weren't going to give up an inch of ground.

We put two machine guns on the causeway, and there was water all around us. It was about 1:00 A. M. before all was quiet. Then we began to make plans for an attack at 4:30. We worked out the plans on the map.

We continued the K Company attack the next day. We had the engineer platoon start moving mines from S-9 along the beach road. He worked all night. A machine gun kept him from removing them as fast as he could have otherwise. He had to work on his stomach all the while, but before daylight he got the road pretty well cleared. After daylight he had all the mines out.

Two 57mm. guns were brought down the road from a house to the front lines to the little embankment which we had slept behind. All during the night a machine gun had been firing at the embankment, about two feet over our heads. There were about two hundred and fifty men along that road during the night. We got these 57's up, and I took Lt. Etta and showed him where the two guns were to go—one on the causeway and on behind the embankment. I pointed out the fortifications and told him I wanted the guns to be able to fire on them direct. I also got a tank. The larger guns had been knocked out during the night.

Here we tried to make an attack on them the next morning. We got off about 9:00 A. M. K Company tried to make a flanking attack sometime during the morning. It went through the water and set up a platoon. They were up to their necks in water. They were slaughtered in the water by machine gun fire. Captain Ernest said something had to be done about it. He grabbed a patrol and jumped into the water and yelled at them. He actually took the fire of machine guns from these men, because the Germans fired on him instead.

I ran down the road toward the 57mm. gun. It had ceased firing. Sgt. Thomas was behind the gun. I stuck one or two rounds in the 57 and let go with it. As soon as I fired, back came machine gun fire. Then we got some smoke from 4.2 from Captain Williams and got K Company out of the water—what was left of K Company.

By that time we had cleaned out two or three houses on the beach. It was approximately forty yards of dry beach. We got two machine guns in the houses. They began firing on the fortification about three hundred yards away. I sent a tank up the beach wall and got the bridge reinforced. We did everything possible to get the fortification to surrender, but it did not.

We fought a good part of the day, and in the afternoon when we had practically given up getting it to surrender, there was a fortification near Ravenoville where the Navy claimed they had seen a couple of white flags. We got permission from the regiment, left one company, about half of the mortars, and made a flanking attack with I and L Companies. We went out on the beach and started to Ravenoville.

Coming off this area from the water side from our position there, we had captured about twenty prisoners. Pvt. Meis, in talking to the German staff sergeant and private, found out that they had come from the fortification, which was the one we wanted to take. He stated that some men and two officers had been killed and that they would surrender if we could get to them, provided that one of the officers hadn't taken command. They further said that when the men wanted to surrender the fortification earlier that day and had tried to put up white flags, that the officers had fired on them and that they had fired back.

We kept this German Sergeant and private and made the flanking attack about two miles down the road. Going down the road together were Captain Gatto, Captain Walker, and myself. It was about dusk when we got there. We decided we would send this German private in. We went further and saw a mob of men and so we dropped some smoke and he marched in. About eighty enemy surrendered at this fortification. We got them lined up and singled the one out who knew about mines on the beaches, another who knew about fortifications, and still another who knew about supplies. We left a medic to take care of the wounded. We marched the other men to the Regimental Command Post.

That night, we had the engineer platoon come in and put in a one span bridge over a bomb crater, which had been blown up so that water would flow across the road. During the night we got tanks to come down to our place on the beach. Staying with me that night were Captain Bridgeman, Captain Gatto, Captain Walker, and Captain Huck.

K Company was on the opposite side from us, about a mile away. In between us we had this German fortification from which we had captured prisoners. but which did not surrender. We slept in a blown-up place on the beach wall.

During the night our C-47's were bringing gliders in. Ack-ack went up from the fortification. We fired mortars and silenced them from firing the ack-ack, Next morning we were making plans to assault the place from both sides of the beach. We were ready to begin the assault when I was ordered to report to another place to help ward off an attack. Arrangements were made that the engineers would blow up the pillboxes and houses full of Germans. There were about twenty-five houses there. This was off the causeway from Ravenoville. I started out with the company in formation. I got a few men across the causeway and this fortification opened up with machine guns and fired 20 mm, ack-ack also. We had some casualties. Our machine guns fired at them, but we couldn't get it stopped. I jumped on the side of the platoon sergeant's tank of the 776th Battalion, and told him I was going on the causeway, and I went and lay down and observed where the machine gun fire was coming from. I told him to come along beside me in the tank and adjust his firing. He did so and they directed a great deal of fire. It was hit on all sides. We got off about eight or ten shots from the tank and hit the back door of the fortification. We tried to shoot the entrance. About fifteen Germans ran out and across the field but were stopped after about fifty yards when the tank fired two rounds at them.

Then a fortification, which was so well camouflaged that we hadn't seen it, began to fire. We changed positions and fired at the second fortification. We got off about ten rounds more before they ceased their fire.

I had the tank placed so it could catch any fire, and after I got the men across I jumped on the tank and we got through O. K. Going out we stopped and fired at pillboxes alongside the road.

From *History of the Twenty-Second United States Infantry in World War II,*—compiled and edited by Dr. William Boice.

ABOUT THE AUTHOR

JOSEPH W. "JOE" MCQUAID grew up in Candia, N.H. The son and grandson of newspapermen, he worked four summers (1965–1968) at the Mt. Washington Cog Railway as a teenager. At the same time, he began working winters for his father at the *New Hampshire Sunday News* and later at the daily *Union Leader*, first as office boy and then as a part time sports reporter.

McQuaid became a fulltime news reporter and photographer and was named editor of the *Sunday News* at age 22, working for its co-founder, B.J. McQuaid, and for *Union Leader* and *Sunday News* owner and publisher William Loeb.

McQuaid became managing editor, editor-in-chief, and later publisher of the only statewide newspaper in New Hampshire.

He has covered state and presidential politics and reported on the U.S. military from the Mideast and Europe. In September of 2010, he and *Union Leader* photographer Bob LaPree were embedded in Afghanistan with "Charlie Company," a New Hampshire National Guard combat company.

The winner of numerous awards for his reporting and editorials, McQuaid is a recipient of the Yankee Quill award of the Academy of New England Journalists, recognizing a lifetime contribution toward excellence in journalism in New England.

He is president of the Nackey S. Loeb School of Communications, Inc.

He and his wife, Signe Anderson McQuaid, live in Manchester. Their son, Brendan, is now president of Union Leader Corp. Their daughter, Katharine, oversees the company's marketing.